Praise

'The recruitment of the right people in the right
place, and the retention of them, are fundamental
aims of our charity so that we can provide good
care, consistently. Neil Eastwood knows how the
care sector works at all levels, and applies a practical
approach that empowers teams to overcome
barriers to recruitment and retention and hire with
success and confidence. I've worked with Neil in
my capacity as care entrepreneur and charity chief
executive, where I have witnessed, first-hand, how
his ideas, and the practical execution of them, deliver
tangible results and maintain a positive culture
through change in a wide variety of environments.

The pandemic, demographic change and economic
uncertainty have hit the social care sector hard; this
second-edition grasps the innovation and resilience
developed amid this adversity and translates that into
strategies and plans to flourish.'

— **Steve Allen**, Group Chief Executive,
Friends of the Elderly

'The most important people in any care organisation
are the carers. This timely book focuses on what
I believe is the single most important issue in the
care sector today – how to recruit and retain key
employees.'

— **Trevor Brocklebank**, Co-founder of Rise
and Home Instead UK

'What makes this book so valuable is not only the huge trove of insights and tips, but that they are practical and actionable, not theoretical. It is an invaluable resource for any social care provider and this second edition contains even more advice at a time the sector desperately needs it.'
— **Jayne Davey**, Chief Operating Officer, Voyage Care

'Neil's insight into the conditions that fuel the social care employee crisis – as well as his solutions – are unique. He possesses the rare ability to distil down a huge problem, such as this, and deliver incredibly effective solutions that are not only easy to understand, but also easy to implement in your business. If your business is suffering from the ever-shrinking pool of quality care workers, I *highly* recommend Neil's book *Saving Social Care*. It delivers real world solutions and advice that can mean the difference between surviving and truly succeeding.'
— **Leigh Davis**, Owner, Davis+Delany, Fayetteville, Arkansas, USA

'It is great to see this "Bible" on social care staffing being updated as the information in this book just works. We have applied Neil's approach to our business since the original book was first published several years ago and it has helped us build a national network with a high quality, stable and committed workforce. This book contains everything you need to know. Brimming with straightforward strategies to transform the quality and volume of your care staff. And importantly keep them in the business longer too. Neil really is the subject expert on recruiting and retaining staff in social care.'
— **Ken Deary**, Owner and Chairman, Right At Home UK

'This is a timely update to an already indispensable guide to overcoming the very real recruitment challenges in the caring profession. Those who chose to make this their career pre-pandemic faced unimaginable challenges. Those people also showed us the very best of what it means to be a carer, playing a critical role in maintaining the quality of life of some of the most vulnerable people in our communities. Neil shares practical tools and ideas to attract and recruit staff, but *Saving Social Care* goes beyond that. It is also a handbook to help retain staff, and in doing so, help to truly value the contribution carers make to our society.'
   — **Beverly Futtit**, Chief Executive CAHSC
      Learning Partnership

'For years now Neil Eastwood has been the number one leading voice on recruitment in social care. He knows the social care sector and its challenges and has very practical and insightful answers to the problems we face. Our charity supports care workers that still work in the sector and our beneficiaries are desperate for more colleagues to join them and Neil's brilliant book goes a long way to achieving that. It also helps us raise money towards supporting care workers so a win for social care on all fronts.'
   — **Karolina Gerlich**, Chief Executive Officer,
      The Care Workers' Charity

'I wish *Saving Social Care* had been written while I was involved in managing care and support services. Recruitment and retention are without doubt two of the biggest challenges faced by the social care sector, and probably always have been. The trouble is the problem is getting much worse. Some parts of the care sector have reached crisis point.

It doesn't have to be like this. *Saving Social Care* addresses an alternative narrative exploring the satisfaction that comes from making a difference to people's lives while continuing to learn and develop. The practical focus of this book shows a depth of wisdom gained from hard-earned experience. It is inspirational, and managers who make use of the ideas and guidance will be equipped to transform the services they offer.'
— **Des Kelly** OBE, Former Executive Director, National Care Forum

'I am delighted to see Neil's valuable and practical suggestions updated to recognise the challenges we are facing in Social Care recruitment and retention. After the hard work and determination that our workforce showed throughout Covid-19, it is time to reopen the debate about how to attract and retain the best and Neil's advice is welcome enthusiasm and positivity for an uncertain future.'
— **Jo Land**, VODG Trustee, CEO of Avenues Group

'Neil's understanding of what makes employees tick in social care is second to none. When I have a problem with recruitment and retention, this is my go-to text. Packed full of practical tips and ideas, I cannot recommend this book highly enough.'
— **Sara Livadeas**, Owner, Social Care Works Ltd

'Neil has shared his great pearls of wisdom in this excellent book. Having known Neil from his early days and been fortunate to work with him with our care providers across Surrey over a number of years he has brought a creative, energetic and well researched but very practical and realistic approach to his work. He inspires an "it is possible" approach to this key challenge for all social care providers who face recruitment difficulties, while also highlighting that it's not just a numbers game; quality and suitability of candidates are also key to a sustainable quality care service. A great read and will inspire many more providers to take a fresh look at recruitment.'

— **Erica Lockhart**, Chair, South East Social Care Alliance (SESCA)

'Neil really captures the challenges social care faces in recruiting and retaining the best quality and values-led workforce and goes further to reflect the changed landscape post-pandemic, following the UK's exit from the EU and in the context of a tightening labour market. Any people manager or specialist will appreciate these brilliant insights and simple but effective solutions which in combination make for a really cohesive approach to recruitment and retention.'

— **Caroline Neal**, Director of People and Organisational Development, Avenues Group and Co-Chair, Voluntary Organisations Disability Group HR Network

'The new edition of *Saving Social Care* has been updated to reflect the changes to the landscape that result from the UK leaving the EU, the pandemic, the introduction of Integrated Care Systems and the cumulative effects of year upon year of below-inflation fee rate uplifts.

The wide-ranging ways in which these have impacted the social care workforce mean that knowing about creative ways of approaching candidate attraction, recruitment and retention are more important than ever and *Saving Social Care* is full of useful hints and tips.

This is a must read for any Social Care provider seeking to employ people who have the values and personal characteristics that our sector needs during these challenging times and it's an uplifting read too.'

— **Clive Parry**, England Director, Association for Real Change

'In this new edition of his ground-breaking and indispensable book, Neil has taken his tried and tested blueprint for successful social care recruitment to a whole new level of brilliance. Always ahead of the curve, Neil has adapted this wonderful collection of sensible advice and best practice for the frightening, post-pandemic landscape social care now finds itself in. With care providers now trying to navigate an unprecedented staffing crisis, *Saving Social Care* has never been a more valuable tool in our arsenal.'

— **Mike Padgham**, Chair, Independent Care Group

'I particularly like this book as it is couched in the context of current care settings. It recognises the unique circumstances many employers will find themselves in and does not shy away from recognising the challenges presented by the way in which the outside world views the profession of care. Key factors for me include the recognition and value of an older workforce, the systematic role of new media to attract from within communities, the promotion of the role of data in driving forward retention and recruitment strategies and most importantly the never-ending innovative tips and tricks.

I really believe that this book has something for even the most experienced HR leader – as well as being essential reading for those looking to refresh, revise or develop their recruitment and retention strategy. It is needed now more than ever.'

> — **Professor Vic Rayner** OBE, CEO, National Care
> Forum

'At a time when recruitment and retention are the biggest challenges facing care providers, Neil Eastwood's expert insights on how to overcome the challenges, explained in a practical and easy access way, are invaluable. The latest release of his book is a must read for every director, manager and HR professional working in the care sector who wants their business to thrive.'

> — **James Sage**, Employment Partner, and Head
> of Health & Social Care, RWK Goodman LLP

'Social care is a fundamental part of all our communities, it supports people to live their lives every day and most people who work in social care find it incredibly rewarding. Recruitment and retention remains a complex challenge though, which will be impacting on the lives of people who need social care. This new edition from Neil will get you thinking about what more you could do to attract and keep people with the right values to work in our sector.'

> — **Oonagh Smyth**, CEO, Skills for Care

'Neil remains a leading thinker, teacher and innovator in the field of social care recruitment and retention. His engaging and practical approach has stimulated numerous organisations to up their game as they seek to maintain, develop and grow their workforce.

This new edition offers additional research findings and insights, particularly on the emotional importance and value of caring to those who give as well as receive care. Due to our ageing populations, the gap between supply and demand for care internationally will likely become even more extreme. Countries across the globe are competing for recruits. Those that care for care workers as much as care workers care for the people they support, and embrace technology and other solutions to enhance employee experience, are most likely to succeed.'

— **Dr Jane Townson** OBE, Chief Executive,
    Homecare Association

'Neil Eastwood has crafted a wonderful book that is focused on helping leaders of social care agencies around the world do a better job of finding and keeping workers to care for the elderly and disabled. This is powerful information that will help you overcome the challenges of the global caregiver recruiting and retention crisis.'

— **Stephen Tweed**, CEO, Leading Home Care...
    a Tweed Jeffries company, Louisville, KY USA,
    Founder, Home Care CEO Forum, Federal Way
    Washington, USA, and author of *Conquering the
    Crisis: Proven Solutions for Caregiver Recruiting
    and Retention*

'In a time when recruitment and retention levels are at an all-time low across adult social care, this new edition of Neil's book is greatly welcomed. Anyone who has not experienced Neil's wealth of knowledge and experience is guaranteed to find *Saving Social Care* an irreplaceable resource. As a provider of home care, I have found *Saving Social Care* to be an invaluable source of information and advice.'

— **Melanie Weatherley** MBE, Co-Chair The Care Association Alliance; Chair of Lincolnshire Care Association, and Owner of Walnut Care at Home

'Neil shares his knowledge so accessibly that anyone reading will find his advice invaluable. Neil's huge contribution to recruitment and retention in social care is something that everyone in the sector should be aware of, and taking advantage of all his shared learning and expertise will no doubt be the best decision you can make!'

— **Lisa Werthmann**, Director, Care Management Matters

SECOND EDITION

SAVING SOCIAL CARE

How to find more of the best frontline care
employees and keep the ones you have

NEIL EASTWOOD

Re think

First published in Great Britain 2017
by Rethink Press (www.rethinkpress.com)

This second edition published in 2023

Idea icon by Adrien Coquet from https://thenounproject.com

Disclaimer
This book is not intended to provide legal advice. If you require such advice, please seek the services of a legal provider specialising in human resources in social care.

All author royalties from sales of this book go to The Care Workers Charity (www.thecareworkerscharity.org.uk)

*This book is dedicated to all those who care for and support
the vulnerable in our society, paid or unpaid.
You have my utmost respect.*

Contents

Foreword

Social care was on the frontline of the global Covid-19 pandemic, and social care staff proved themselves to be caring, committed and professional. The pandemic also showed the skills and competencies of our amazing staff – many things that were thought to be the remit of medical staff in the NHS were being ably carried out by social care professionals. The pandemic also put enormous stress on our staff and, because of government policy, as well as the enormous pressures they were facing, some staff have left the sector. This has exacerbated the challenges facing care services. As well as the post-pandemic issues, there is the ever-present need to secure better funding; there is the complex nature of the work; and there is the fact that the people we support have increasingly high levels of dependency and complex needs. We are in a regulated sector and are all trying to improve quality and make our services more effective and efficient to deliver better outcomes. But the consequences of making a mistake can not only be devastating for service users but can also destroy the lives and careers of the people who work in care. We need to see a regulatory system that is the cornerstone of sector improvement.

The most important resource in any care service is the staff. Everything we are trying to achieve hinges on having the right people with the right attitudes and values who are committed to delivering the highest quality care. Care work is a complicated job and the big challenge for any organisation is recruiting and retaining the right staff. We must then train, nurture and support them so that they want to stay within the organisation and the sector.

The demographics are clear. They tell us that we will need far more people in social care, but at the same time as the need is increasing, the numbers of people entering the workforce is in steady decline. The uncertainties post-Brexit and the pandemic leave us unclear about how we will recruit the next generation of care staff.

Neil Eastwood has produced a comprehensive and practical guide on how to recruit and retain a high-quality workforce, and many answers to big questions are contained within this book. What I love about Neil's approach is that he does not shy away from the enormous challenges in the sector, instead clearly articulating them right from the start of this compelling book. He then tackles these challenges head-on and gives a range of practical insights and tips on how to ensure there is a clear and consistent approach within your organisation to recruiting and retaining a high-quality workforce.

Neil is cognisant of the way in which social care is perceived and offers clear views about how we need to shift the perceptions of social care from a low-skilled occupation where some staff abuse the people in their care. Social care needs to be acknowledged and recognised, and the staff who work in the sector must receive the same degree of support as our colleagues in the NHS.

Neil highlights that social care is an engine of economic growth; hopefully, this will change the views of politicians and the public about its importance to everyone, not just those who currently use it.

Saving Social Care is a publication that you can constantly revisit. The clarity and simplicity of many of the suggestions help to frame a coherent approach to recruitment and retention within your organisation, and the messages in this book are as appropriate for the large multi-site provider as they are for the small service. Neil has proved that a clear and consistent approach to recruitment and retention is available to everybody, not just those with mature or large infrastructures.

The book also offers practical advice about such elements as interviews. What's extra helpful is that Neil suggests follow-up questions that will test applicants' answers and verify whether they are suitable and have the right values for and expectations of the role they are applying for.

Saving Social Care is an essential read for anybody who is recruiting and supporting staff in a social care service, but it is also relevant to those who are working or thinking of working in the sector. It will help them to focus on their career to date and think about what they need in terms of support to meet their career goals.

This is one of the best and most accessible books I have read on recruitment and retention. It's a vital resource for any care provider.

Professor Martin Green OBE
Chief Executive,
Care England

Preface to the Second Edition

It is six years since *Saving Social Care* was first published and an extraordinary amount has happened since then. Recruitment and retention were already a major concern for employers; now, after the Covid-19 pandemic ravaged the sector and the UK exited the EU, it has become firmly entrenched as an existential threat for the foreseeable future.

As I re-read my book, I was struck by how much of it has stood the test of time. The fundamentals of finding and keeping a caring workforce have not changed. But six years on, I wanted to include not only my latest research and thinking but also discuss the impact of recent events, including Covid-19, Brexit and the global workforce shortage that is affecting every social care employer. I have also significantly expanded the text on retention to explore the unique psychological pull of care work and how we can use this to improve job satisfaction and, thus, retention.

In my travels around the UK and further afield, I have met many people who have read the book. I even once saw someone reading a copy on the London Underground but was too bashful to introduce myself.

I hope this new edition continues to help recruiters and managers navigate the now even choppier waters of social care recruitment and retention.

Introduction

Back in 2009, when I wasn't paying enough attention, my healthcare career veered off course and landed me unceremoniously in the social care sector. Despite numerous opportunities to escape – some very inviting, come to think of it – I have stayed. The National Health Service's frumpy and rather large sister turned out to be fascinating company.

Social care in the UK employs hundreds of thousands more people than her more glamourous sibling and performs a role so critical, so core to what defines human decency, that life without her is unthinkable. It's the same around the world. Despite all this, the social care workforce remains hugely underrated and puts up with high levels of responsibility, low pay, and a lack of respect from wider society.

So, who are these over 1.5 million souls across the UK (and many more millions internationally) caring for people they are not related to and whom they have never previously met? What motivates them when there are so many more 'comfortable' alternatives? It is true, for some it is 'just a job', but the majority, over 60% of care workers intentionally choose this work because they enjoy helping others, deeply value the relationships with those they care for and have a desire to do something meaningful with their time.[1]

The more I investigated, the more I discovered that, for the right type of person, the intrinsic rewards of hands-on care, and in many cases the opportunity to work with likeminded organisations and individuals, are so strong that they manage to overcome challenging conditions and poor perceptions, and in so doing keep this vital service afloat.

But as people are living longer, demand for paid care is rising relentlessly and the labour market is tightening. Fewer young people are choosing to be care workers. We are facing a care gap.

That is a scary prospect for our society, but for care employers it is a looming crisis. The current ways of finding and keeping effective care staff are not good enough. They are no longer delivering anywhere near sufficient numbers of quality applicants who make it through their first year. To make matters worse, staff retention rates are getting unhealthier year by year, requiring even more recruiting effort just to stand still.

But, as I have witnessed from my thirteen years of investigation, a handful of care providers around the world have found clever ways to seek out, attract, screen, select, mentor, and support their workforce. It turns out there are actually enough of the right types of people in the communities around us, if we know where to look and what to say when we find them. Equally important are simple, effective, and low-cost ways of avoiding unsuitable applicants, making the good ones feel welcome and keeping them for longer.

This book brings all that know-how together in a practical, accessible and actionable format. There isn't one right way to recruit and retain, so I have shared a range of interventions and advice and you'll need to test and tweak to find what's best in your situation. Every single one of the methods and tips included here have already inspired and transformed many care businesses. I hope they do the same for you.

Who is this book for?

This book is for anyone with an interest in or tasked with recruiting and retaining a quality frontline care workforce. Typically, this will include owners, directors, managers and in-house recruiters with a homecare agency, residential care or nursing home, supported living or live-in care provider. It also has value for consumers and their families taking this daunting job on themselves. As well as practitioners, it is relevant for workforce planning and social services professionals in local or central government with a social services responsibility. It is also applicable to the healthcare sector.

The text is written with a UK audience in mind, but many of the recommendations will work just as well in any country with a paid social care workforce.

Saving Social Care is based on thirteen years of research and best practice review, not only in the UK but the USA, Australia, Europe and other countries. I have strong opinions about which approaches work and which don't, as you will discover.

Terminology

Care workers. For purposes of this book, a care worker is my catch-all term for any employed frontline care or support role. This could be within an aged care, disability, family or youth environment. A care worker is defined as someone who performs certain functions related to the care or support of another in a professional, paid capacity. These include hands-on care, such as personal care, bathing and dressing, social tasks such as companionship, meal preparation, and help to maintain an individual's independence.

For simplicity, I use the term 'care worker' to encompass a range of care and support roles in a variety of care settings, including the client's own home, unless expressly stated otherwise. I use the term 'carer' when referring to those performing unpaid care (most commonly those who care for a loved one).

Those receiving care or support. When referring to those receiving care or support, I tend to use the term 'consumer'. These individuals can be known by many other names, such as service users, clients, residents, customers or people being supported, but for brevity I will mostly stick with consumers.

Applicants or candidates. I attempt to maintain the convention that an applicant is someone who has applied to your organisation while a candidate is someone accepted by you into your recruitment funnel, but they are almost interchangeable.

Care provider. An organisation employing staff to provide care or support to vulnerable individuals. This can be a state-owned, not-for-profit or for-profit entity.

PART ONE
RECRUITING WELL

Not only its growth, but the ongoing existence of every care provider will ultimately be determined by the effectiveness of its recruitment strategies and operation.

1
Powerful Headwinds

Recruiting care workers has become fiendishly hard, which is perhaps something you already know from bitter experience. Candidates are unpredictable and so are the results of recruitment efforts. Sometimes your efforts deliver more applicants than you expected, then the next week, nothing. The care provider in the neighbouring territory seems to rely on methods that completely bomb out for you. Regardless, the quality of those applicants seems to be getting gradually worse.

Part of the reason for this local variation (and a lot of the reason why recruitment is hard for everyone) is that the social care recruitment market is exposed to a diverse range of powerful external factors, most of which aren't all that helpful. These headwinds can seem hurricane-force since the Coronavirus pandemic of 2019. Let's start by unpicking what the major forces bearing down on your organisation are. I will also suggest some potential remedies to these headwinds where I can, but since most require governmental policy change, or wide agreement from a range of stakeholders with different agendas, or a large amount of money and effort, I don't think we should wait around for the cavalry to come charging over the hill anytime soon. It is far better to take control – and that's what this book is all about.

Demographics

If you work in social care, you, like me, will have sat through countless presentations where the opening slides, or even the entire presentation, describe the unstoppable ageing of our society and the demands this will place on the search for workers. Particularly the younger, working-age, female demographic in countries like the UK, who make up the bulk of the workforce in this sector, will not grow at anywhere near the level needed to service future demand for frontline workers. Those same workers are also coveted by other employers, not just in social care but also retail, hospitality and, of course, healthcare. At the same time, demand for care has jumped as a result of the mental and physical impact of Covid-19.

So, societal ageing is fuelling a large and growing demand for frontline care workers, turbocharged by the aftermath of the pandemic, while the traditional workforce is not keeping pace and prospective and current care workers are being enticed to leave to better paid and less demanding alternatives. Not an encouraging place to start, but if you look a little deeper, there are some big opportunities to approach this challenge differently.

This ageing trend is also creating a high-potential future care workforce, particularly the economically active 60-69-year-olds. In the UK, this group is projected to grow over 30% in the next ten years, driven by the growth of women participating in the labour force.[2]

In many cases, these older potential workers have not made adequate pension provision as generous final salary company schemes ends and life expectancy increases, and therefore will be motivated to take on flexible local work. Or they might simply be bored and want to seek out meaningful part-time employment. Better health in older age will support not just a desire but an ability to work.

Later we will look at how to make care work appealing to this group, where to look for them in the community and how to make them feel valued. But much more central- and local-government support to convince older people of the value of a paid care role would be welcomed. Thus far, government national awareness campaigns have repeatedly targeted a younger demographic.

A changing society

Attitudes and social norms have been changing. Harvard professor, Robert Putnam, documented this phenomenon powerfully in his influential book *Bowling Alone*,[3] where he analysed huge data sets to demonstrate how Americans are becoming increasingly disconnected from social structures, such as churches and clubs, and are increasingly less likely to be involved in their communities, or even have dinners as a family.

This weakening of social bonds, which we can see evidence of in most Western societies, be it in the decline in church congregations, changing work practices with the growth of short-term contracts or a lack of tolerance stemming from increased tribalism, is bad news for social care recruiters. We rely on building a workforce that does their job for more than simply financial rewards. The less able or prepared our future candidate pool is to engage with neighbours and communities in general, the harder our job will be.

Addressing what Putnam calls a 'reduction in social capital' will be a major challenge and requires bold action. One intervention that I want to see is the introduction of a period of compulsory community service for young people (also known in some countries as Civilian Service) so they get early exposure to the intrinsic rewards of helping others, which has been lost with the rise of social media. I chose this option at school in the early 1980s instead of enlisting in the Combined Cadet Force and never forgot the wonderful older people I met and helped. I also never forgot the weekly jeering of my peers in their military fatigues, who I expect to come around to understanding the value of social care in about twenty years' time.

The role of technology

The rise of smartphones, the internet and social media all play a strong role in fostering a younger generation less familiar with face-to-face relationships as their primary means of communication and generating an expectation of instant gratification and constant stimulation. We can see the impact of this change in the gradual but relentless decline in under twenty-fives choosing social care as a career. For example, The King's Fund and Skills for Care have recorded a fall in the percentage of under twenty-fives in social care roles in each of the past nine years.[4]

Technology may ultimately contribute to resolving social care's supply-side challenges, for example by displacing whole categories of jobs, particularly those with a high percentage of predictable physical activities such as professional driving as well those in 'bricks and mortar' retail shops. Whether those surplus workers would make suitable and willing frontline care staff is another matter entirely, of course, but there is no doubt very few workers can be certain of long-term employment in the same occupation as technology disrupts the workplace. Ironically, the growth of demand in care roles could provide much of the job security currently lacking in many traditional roles being disrupted by technology.

Public perceptions

Hands-on caring can be seen by those without direct exposure to it as menial, low paid and emotionally and physically demanding. It is also, from the outside at least, tarnished with a narrative of decline, suffering and death.

As if that wasn't enough to depress the most optimistic public relations professional, the UK national media's portrayal of care staff through high-profile investigative current affairs programmes such as BBC Panorama's 'Undercover Care: The Abuse Exposed' (2011), 'Behind Closed Doors: Elderly Care Exposed' (2014), 'Nursing Homes Undercover' (2016) and 'Undercover Hospital: Patients at Risk' (2022) stays long in the public memory.

At a local level, a regular drip-feed of news headlines publicising the few delinquent care staff who steal from or abuse their vulnerable clients continues to reinforce a challenging recruitment environment. The sector has made some attempts to drive a positive news agenda, but structural challenges and the preference of the media for negative sensational news stories has made this largely ineffectual.

Social care in England needs to make it much clearer to the public that it is an equal partner to the NHS. My recommendation is that care settings be able to use a 'working in partnership with the NHS' strapline to identify and bring together what are now thousands of independent small businesses. This branding will go some way to raising the profile of the sector in the mind of the public and help give confidence to wavering applicants for whom working for a familiar name brings respect and confidence.

In today's culture, we should not overlook the role of celebrity endorsement. A media campaign highlighting the importance of care fronted by high-profile respected individuals would be a good start.

Policy challenges

The willingness to care for others does not receive enough recognition by policymakers, despite the huge contribution it makes to social cohesion and reducing suffering in society. The lauding of academic achievement, through the prioritisation of degrees over vocational education, has, in my view, hugely damaged both healthcare and social care and sent a corrosive message to a generation of potential front-line care staff.

A specific example is the 2009 UK Government policy announcement that nurses would need a degree-level qualification from 2013. Closing the door to caring, relationship-centric and perfectly able hands-on practitioners in favour of educational achievers was an unfortunate decision. Being academically clever is not the opposite of caring, but I would bring back state-enrolled nurses, a career pathway we can still see across much of Europe. I can only hope that some of those thousands of compassionate young people who are turned away each year consider social care as a career.

Other policy areas of note are the reform of in-work benefits to remove restrictions on hours worked, the reform of pension taxes to encourage active retirees to return to work, improvements to family carer benefits and subsidised, or free, childcare for social care workers.

Structural challenges

In England, the for-profit and voluntary sector provision in social care has grown since the 1990s to employ almost nine out of ten workers[5] across over 17,900 organisations where once local authorities employed almost all care staff. While the outsourcing of social care on such a large scale has delivered major financial savings for the public sector, this level of market fragmentation has made recruitment and retention of frontline staff harder for individual providers.

First, with so many providers (those 17,900 organisations operate through over 39,000 sites in England alone) there is intense competition for staff. This pits providers against each other and restricts collaboration, such as joint recruitment activity, or the sharing of recruitment best practices. Second, with multiple employers funding similar infrastructures with which to attract, select and train new staff, there is high-cost duplication and a lack of economies of scale, such as the buying power to negotiate preferential rates with internet job boards or recruitment agencies. I estimate almost 70% of care providers do not employ a dedicated recruiter, which leads to inefficiencies and a poor candidate experience.

There is some sporadic evidence of local collaborations, often driven by a funder such as a local authority, which can play the role of market-shaper, but overall, recruiters work in isolation and see nearby providers as competitors, not potential allies in the search for talent. For example, where is the incentive for providers to pass high-potential candidates, who live a little too far away, to a closer employer? There is also often weak collaboration and poor communication between local NHS bodies and social care providers in England, although the emergence of integrated care systems is a positive step.

Despite moves toward integrating social care and healthcare in England, wholesale reform of social care funding in the UK is long overdue, although it will be a very long time before changes impact recruitment and retention, if at all. A more achievable improvement in England would be to introduce registration of care staff, such as has been implemented in Northern Ireland, Wales and Scotland. Registration will professionalise the role, improve the standing of care workers and boost public confidence. This, however, should not be attempted without first delivering a significant pay rise.

Competition for staff from other sectors

The combination of Covid-19 and Brexit has meant competition from other sectors has intensified. The social care workforce is dominated by females (approximately 85% of all frontline staff) on low wages, and it must compete not only with other care providers but also other lower-skilled service sector employers that seek a similar demographic profile, such as cleaning, food preparation, retail and hospitality. In many cases, unless the worker has a 'calling' to care for others, then these substitute job opportunities can be more appealing, offering similar or superior rates of pay for better working conditions.

Improvements in the status of the social care workforce would help make care work more attractive. In most cases, though, if a job seeker is ambivalent about caring for others, then no amount of sweeteners will address the fundamental lack of a calling. Even if they join, most don't stay, with Skills for Care identifying a staff turnover of 39.9% for those with less than a year's service and my own research identifying between 43–50% of new starters leaving in the first twelve months where there is not a prior connection with either the employer, a care worker or a values-match.[6] But by using creative recruitment-sourcing techniques, as I discuss in this book, there will be access to enough suitable prospective employees to overcome this challenge.

Funding pressures

Approximately 53% of care home places[7] and 58% of homecare in the UK is funded by local authorities,[8] where the fee to providers is regulated and can be subject to competitive tender. Funding pressures since 2010 have seen repeated reductions in these fee levels, or smaller annual increases that fail to keep pace with the costs incurred by providers. This cap limits the hourly rates providers can pay their staff.

We will discuss the role of pay in detail later. Although it is not a primary motivator for the genuinely caring frontline employee, it certainly affects the perceived attractiveness of the role to prospective care workers and, therefore, influences the number of applications, particularly from those seeking a job on, for example, an internet job board where employers compete in an online marketplace. Rises in the cost of living have increased calls for significant improvements in pay rates. Pay rises for NHS staff, however well-deserved, can create even more dissatisfaction in the care sector.

Reform of the funding of health and social care in the UK, particularly England, is long overdue, despite repeated white and green papers and consultations. Rather than attempt to address this complex issue here I would direct readers to the admirable work of the Health Foundation[9] and The King's Fund,[10] both voices of objectivity and reason in these matters.

Employment costs rising

The introduction of the National Living Wage in the UK in 2016 has, in most areas of the country, increased the wage bill of social care providers. Of course, ensuring that care staff are paid adequately is a positive step, but since this increase applied to all employment sectors, there is no differentiation to favour frontline care roles, which makes social care no more attractive than other low-wage jobs, relatively speaking.

Enabling providers to fund fair rates of pay for staff is tied to the funding debate in social care, but as more and more of those requiring care are self-funding, so providers have more flexibility in setting fees at a level where care staff can be better paid. We have already seen this with clear evidence of residential care home providers subsidising local authority-funded residents by increasing the fees for those paying privately.[11]

Given the importance of the sector, there should be a 'caring supplement' to the Living Wage, with pass-through funding from social services. This would send a powerful message about the value of front-line care to society (see Chapter 14 and Appendix 1 for why simply relying on pay increases to 'solve' our recruitment and, particularly, retention challenges is a mistake.) The UK pays approximately 69% of the average national hourly wage to care workers.[12] To match the top EU countries, this should increase by approximately 25%, but it would be a real challenge to implement fairly across the many thousands of independent businesses that make up the sector.

The economy and local labour market conditions

In many parts of the country, particularly in areas where there is easy commuting into London, or large local substitute employers, it has been harder for care employers to compete using traditional recruitment methods.

Across the country, the recruitment market for social care waxes and wanes with the economic conditions. You could take the view that social care benefits from recessionary conditions since more workers are available and willing to consider this type of work.

Again, making a career in care more attractive can help the sector weather periods of high employment, but a more viable solution is to encourage those who we have identified as having the values we seek, including those not in the labour market, such as active retirees, young people and family carers, to consider frontline care. This is a fundamental change we must make, since if you have a calling to care you are not only much more likely to join our sector, but you are much more resilient once you are here.

Summary

- There is no doubt social care faces an unprecedented range of challenges, but there is also much cause for optimism.

- We must start communicating the intrinsic rewards of care work more widely and creatively.

- Social care deserves a much higher profile and more recognition for those who work in it. There is too much talent, energy and passion in the sector for that not to happen in the coming months and years, if we all work together.

2
Picking Your Ideal Target Worker

The starting point for a successful recruitment strategy is being clear about what an ideal candidate for your vacancy looks like – and making sure your colleagues and staff all know and are looking for people displaying the correct qualities.

Fortunately, if you are an established care provider with an existing workforce, you will already have members of staff whom your organisation considers high performers. A great starting point is to identify them and understand as much about them as you can – what values and behaviours do they display? How did they hear about care work and your organisation? Why not ask them, 'How can we find more people like you?'

Time spent talking to your staff is extremely valuable: are there any common themes amongst them, for example previous experience of caring for a loved one, similar life stages, well-developed emotional maturity? Perhaps they live in the same areas. You also might find it instructive to talk to the poorer performing staff members and see if there are patterns that emerge that could influence where you avoid sourcing staff from in future, for example.

The ideal frontline care employee

There is a recurring set of traits or characteristics that are cited by care providers to describe why a member of staff is so good at their job. The list can be quite long, but the following appear regularly:

- A mature outlook, particularly 'emotional maturity'

- Patience

- Empathy / sensitivity to others' needs

- A strong work ethic

- Reliability

- Honesty

- Compassion

- An ability to follow the rules

- Tough-mindedness and strength of character

- Resilience and ability to handle stress

- Introversion (particularly for support worker roles)

- Problem-solvers

- A 'calling' to the work

When I run recruitment workshops with care managers and recruiters, I ask them to come to the session having identified one or two profiles of their highest-performing staff, as we will discuss in Chapter 14. In every case so far, the most popular profile in the session always features an older person (often over fifty). Where younger people (under twenty-fives) feature, they are described as having a maturity beyond their years, and often some exposure to caring for others, such as having a sibling with a disability, has brought them to the sector.

Why do older people make high-performing care workers?

For the avoidance of doubt, let me be clear that young people are desperately needed in caring roles, and when you meet one who is successful in their role, they can be inspirational. But academic and workplace research tells us, time and time again that, with the exception of student nurses and those with a calling or unusual emotional maturity for their age, older workers consistently make better frontline staff. Here are a few of the reasons why.

- **More maturity and life experience.** As people age, their temperament tends to improve, and they are better able to put hardships into perspective. Having more than likely experienced illness, ageing and perhaps the death of a loved one, they have empathy with the frail and vulnerable. Older workers may well have parents who now need support themselves.

- **Require less supervision.** Older workers are less likely to need support as they have confidence relating to others. This is particularly advantageous in a homecare setting.

- **Lower job mobility.** Many older workers have had a career and do not wish to start another. Also, as people age, they tend to settle in an area and put down roots, so are less likely to move for a new role. They also favour local work.

- **Fewer financial needs.** There is considerable financial pressure for those raising children on low incomes; this can encourage them to move job for a better pay rate and limit their resources to manage life shocks like a failure of transport, childcare or sudden expenditure.

- **Lower expectations.** Early in a person's working life there are often high expectations about the future and what they expect from their job. This can reduce as fewer working years remain.

- **Greater investment in the job.** Because the intrinsic rewards of frontline care are generally more readily appreciated by emotionally mature workers, they are often more invested in care work as they place a higher value than younger workers on these aspects.

Many of the preferred characteristics listed are a mix of personality traits, values and workplace attitudes, all of which can be assessed during the recruitment process, as we will see in Chapter 5. In addition to capturing these characteristics, I investigate both how care workers heard about the organisation and their motivation: what made them want to work in this profession? We will look later at the question of why where you go to find applicants is such a powerful predictor of subsequent success in the job.

Motivation

Next let's consider how motivation can affect care outcomes. Because of the perceived low barriers to entry for a frontline care job (basic language qualifications, no experience required, full training provided and pages of situations vacant), it does present itself as a last-resort employment option for some people who are completely unsuitable for the role. The lack of other job opportunities is a poor reason to work in this sector; wanting to help others or enjoying being with older people or those with a disability is a much better starting point. Ideally, you want applicants who are running to you and not running away from something else or treating the role as a temporary stop-gap gig.

The powerful impact of a worker's motivation on the quality of care they deliver was illustrated in research by a team at Northwestern University School of Medicine in 2012.[13] They recorded the motivations of ninety-eight paid care staff and identified three primary motivations: 61% decided to become care workers because they enjoyed being with older people; 31% were unable to find other work; and 8% chose it as a prerequisite to a career in healthcare.

The team then went on to investigate the incidence of falls with fractures amongst those being cared for by each type of care worker in a homecare setting. The difference was marked: clients with care workers who cited job characteristics as their motivation reported almost two-and-a-half times as many falls and fractures as the ones who were cared for by those motivated by love.

The motivation of a paid care worker also has an impact on how long they stay in the role, as we will see in Chapter 13.

 Tip: Watch my whiteboard video 'Why Motivation Matters' at www.savingsocialcare.com/videos

Demographics

From my work with care providers, I've concluded there are five demographic profiles into which most care workers will fit. As we saw from the output of my workshop sessions, older workers (or, perhaps more correctly, those with emotional maturity) are often correlated with success in care, but high-performing staff can be found in each of these demographic groups.

Let's learn a bit more about each of them. We will return to this topic in Chapter 3 when we look at how we can market a job in care and your organisation more effectively to job seekers.

Primary breadwinner and/or single parent

This group is a mainstay of the care sector in most Western societies. Likely to be juggling more than one job or in receipt of state benefits, which could restrict their hours, they have limited resources and lack a support structure. As a result, they are at high risk of being impacted by challenges in their personal life, such as an unreliable car, failed childcare arrangements or financial problems.

Although their focus is often on financial reward because of their circumstances, there are many examples of very committed and successful care workers from this group.

Under-twenty-five

Younger workers mostly include those who choose care work as a stepping-stone to a career in healthcare, but can also include school leavers, university students and the urban professional with a social conscience, perhaps attracted to the voluntary sector or support work. They are less likely to stay in a frontline role, either leaving to further their career, exiting the sector altogether or seeking a management position. Although this group makes up about 8% of UK households,[14] they are concentrated in large urban areas.

From my research, there are several similarities that crop up repeatedly when I enquire about high-performing younger care workers. They are usually either studying for a health or medical career; strongly influenced by older people such as grandparents; have been in care themselves; have a parent working in social care; have a track record of volunteering; have a sibling or a parent they have provided care for; and/or have a gregarious and cheerful personality.

Homemaker

This demographic group has settled down and seeks flexible local work that fits with other commitments. They more commonly live in the suburbs or rurally and will work in frontline care because they enjoy it and its convenience.

Critically, the homemaker needs to feel appreciated for the work she or he does, and although they will get a lot of that from those they care for, they expect their employer to recognise their contribution as well.

Active retiree

As people reach later life and their career is in the past, they are more likely to become involved in the community and find roles, often unpaid, to give something back. At the same time, they want to replace the social interaction they have lost by retiring or from children leaving home.

This group gains a lot from a care role as they stay active, meet new people and feel valued. The challenges lie in reaching them in the community and encouraging them to learn a new skill. One of the aftershocks of Covid-19 in the UK has been the loss from the workforce of over 380,000 over-fifties.[15] It is time to bring them back into care work.

Migrant worker

Migrants can be broadly split into two groups: already here and those you bring from overseas. In the UK, there are large groups of migrants, often in the cities, although due to Brexit and Covid-19, these have reduced significantly. They are a particularly mobile workforce and so are at a higher risk of leaving the area and employment with you. They have a generally good reputation in the care sector as hard-working and reliable staff.

This group is sought after by competing sectors such as hospitality and agriculture, and if they have a partner locally, they may be at risk of leaving because of their partner's changing work commitments.

Bringing care workers into the country under migration visa scheme rules has grown in popularity in recent years, despite the cost and administrative effort as well as the pastoral support required to help them settle. This is a rapidly changing area, so I would encourage you to refer to the Skills for Care website (www.skillsforcare.org.uk) for up-to-date information. I will return to migrant workers in Chapter 11.

As we saw earlier, in order to grow the caring workforce by the numbers required, we can't rely on the traditional demographic group of females between the ages of twenty-five and fifty; we must engage other major under-represented population cohorts. In addition to those covered above, the long list of groups with enough scale to deliver new care workers in volumes also includes men, the unemployed and family carers. Migrants, older workers and family carers are more practical prospects for an individual employer with limited resources to consider.

 Tip: Check out my whiteboard video 'Common Demographic Groups of Care Staff' at www.savingsocialcare.com/videos

Active versus passive job seekers

It took me thirteen years, but finally it dawned on me that we only see two types of applicants in social care: active job seekers and passive job seekers. First, let's dig a bit further into what an active job seeker is, and then see how this fits our requirements in social care.

An active job seeker is... actively looking for a job. So far, so obvious. But what makes people look for a new job? There can be benign reasons – recently moved to the area, returning to work after children, seeking promotion and so on – but there are a lot of potentially negative reasons too. Are they job hoppers? Are they unemployable? Perhaps they feel underpaid? Could they be in dispute with their current employer or recently dismissed? Are they grudgingly looking to protect their benefit payments? Certainly, a qualified frontline care or support worker who can't readily find employment in the sector raises questions.

Compare this to a passive job seeker, that is someone not actively looking for a job. Passive job seekers are those who would make high-potential frontline staff but need to be approached or are happy in their current paid or unpaid care role. They probably do not have an up-to-date CV and are blissfully unaware of your job advert or recruitment drive.

The majority of active job seekers will visit one or more internet job boards, where they are likely to apply for many jobs at a time. This creates a huge screening challenge for recruiters, who have no relationship or connection to the applicant, just a CV or application form on which to identify high-potential applicants. If your recruitment strategy just focuses on active job seekers, you are in trouble. It's becoming increasingly important for employers to widen their recruitment reach to encompass both active and passive applicants, testing as many sources as possible to maximise their chances of identifying quality new staff.

 Tip: Watch my whiteboard video 'Active and Passive Job Seekers' at www.savingsocialcare.com/videos

 Tip: Ensure your recruitment process is not discriminatory. James Sage, Employment Partner in RWK Goodman LLP and Head of Health and Social Care has provided some guidance in Appendix 3.

Summary

- Identify what characteristics your best staff have.

- Ask your best staff how to find more people like them.

- Always ask why each applicant wants to work in care and look for signs of emotional maturity.

- Diversify your recruitment effort to target both active and passive job seekers.

3
Marketing To Both Active And Passive Job Seekers

A good chunk of what makes recruiting successful in any sector is marketing. In fact, if you have a colleague responsible for marketing, which some larger providers and those focused on self-funded clients sometimes do, it is time to be their new best friend. For most of the rest of us in the care sector, marketing can be a mystery and viewed with some bewilderment, but for recruiters it can be the difference between lots of suitable applicants and none.

Let's find out why.

How marketing helps a social care recruiter

To sell anything (like a job or career) to a customer (your new employee) you need to give potential buyers (your applicants) some compelling reasons to want it (their why). This is certainly the case for your ideal target customers (your soon-to-be great care workers) because they will also be coveted by your competitors (any other local employer offering similar roles).

Marketing disciplines and processes help social care recruiters in three important ways:

- They help us appeal to our target audiences by helping us understand their needs and expectations.

- They increase success rates by enhancing the candidate experience.

- They grow our reputation by building our local employer brand.

Let's consider each element in turn and how we can use it to improve our approach to recruitment.

Appealing to our target audience

We looked at how to define who our target audience is in Chapter 2, but there doesn't have to be just one target group. In fact, there are more likely to be several.

First, however, we need to put ourselves in the position of a potential applicant from each target audience group and attempt to make our job as appealing as possible to them by satisfying their employment needs or wants.

More simply put, we need to solve their problem. This is best illustrated by looking at the concerns or goals of different types of potential applicants, as shown on the following page.

Some may not be looking for work. In fact, I would argue that the majority now fall into that category. We must first find them and then sell two things, if they are new to care: our company and the job role. What we say matters because if we can't appeal to their needs, we won't get their attention and the rest of our message will be wasted.

Concern, problem or goal	Examples of who might think this
'Who would ever employ me?'	• Parent returning to work • Mid-life redundancy • Family carer • Victim of domestic abuse in temporary accommodation
'I need work with flexible hours'	• Single parent • Parent with school-age children • Younger person with a portfolio of jobs
'I don't have any skills'	• Parent returning to work • Family carer
'I need to pay the bills'	• Primary breadwinner
'I feel unfulfilled in my current job'	• Anyone working in an 'emotionless' role, such as administration, who seeks a connection with people or more purpose
'What can I do with all this time on my hands?'	• Previous carer for a loved one who has died • Retiree • Economically inactive
'All the jobs are too far to commute/I really hate commuting'	• Rural or village-based
'I miss working with people'	• Recent retiree • Ex-care worker who has taken a better paid role outside the sector
'I want to feel valued and give something back to society'	• Active retiree • Fifty-five+ year old
'I don't feel appreciated in my job'	• Existing paid care worker • Most employees!

Many recruiters make the mistake of ignoring these needs and writing a job advert to try and interest as many people as possible. By doing so, they end up appealing to no one. Here are a few examples of different advertising sources and how each can influence the types of candidates you find there, along with some thoughts on what you need to say.

Internet job boards

Even for high-traffic job sites like internet job boards, we can know some specific things about the people who will look at our advert. They are active job seekers, so they probably need work soon. This could mean they are unemployed, unhappy or want more money. They might be new to the area.

They are probably, although not always, younger, as job boards are more popular with the under thirty-fives. They will be mostly searching by role, so they probably have a specific job in mind already. They will also have a clear target location, because most job seekers for unqualified roles will want local work. The call to action on a job board is also the same for all – an 'Apply' button.

How can you differentiate yourself as an employer on a job board? The rate of pay is one way, although with the National Living Wage in the UK lifting the lowest wage rates, this has reduced (and some recruiters hugely overstate the real pay rate anyway). Others are your perks and benefits, how well you sell your brand and the tone of voice you use.

Apart from these elements, it will come down to visibility, and that means regular re-posting and spending increasing amounts of money to make your advert more visible. Just the same as your competitors are doing.

Facebook

We'll see later why this is still the social media platform to concentrate on, but briefly, if your job advert has been shared or liked by a member of staff on Facebook then there will be some personal connection with the potential applicant, and that can be a powerful endorsement.

If you are using Facebook's targeted advertising service, then your advert is probably going to be viewed on a mobile phone for a second or less as the recipient scrolls through their newsfeed. This means imagery, ideally video, and a snappy headline (and a sprinkling of hashtags, apparently) are critical to gain their attention. You will know a lot about the viewer anyway as you will have specified a location, age range and perhaps interests.

Card in local shop window

Let's say you choose a shop with a catchment area covering a housing estate where several of your staff already live. The demographics are probably quite clear, so your headline should reflect that by appealing to their needs. Also emphasise the local nature of the work by naming your location or specific areas where you can offer work, since you know exactly where your potential applicants live.

Matching candidate expectations

Candidates, like any consumers, are raising their expectations. As technology delivers instant gratification at the tap of a touchscreen, tolerance of delay or lack of communication is lower and the experience of applying for a frontline social care job appears more and more unsexy, clunky and old-fashioned. We must sharpen up our act and fast.

Of course, police checks are in-built delays largely out of a recruiter's control, but much else is within our capability to improve. What we need to focus on is the candidate experience – how the candidate is engaged and enthused.

Increase success rates

First, put yourself in the shoes of a candidate, especially one actively applying for a range of jobs. Imagine how many times you will be asked for the same personal information. Much of it is on your CV, which you have already uploaded. You are going to get data submission fatigue quickly. Many employers ask for far too much information too early in the process, so applicants can often give up before submitting an application. Care providers do need to put some early hurdles in the way to filter out timewasters, but making the application form excruciating is not the hurdle I have in mind. A high-handed approach sends a message to applicants that they have to dance to the employer's tune. This is a poor message to be giving – especially if this is the first impression your applicant receives. It also doesn't acknowledge that candidates now have all the power. They know you need them more than they need you.

Now, let's consider a common first point of contact for candidates over which you have total control: your website. This must be mobile device-optimised so prospective applicants checking it on the move can easily find the 'Careers' or 'Work for us' section and don't need to zoom in to read the text. Next, consider how many clicks, keystrokes or taps it takes to identify and apply for a role with you. Applicants should be able to reach a job application form in three taps/ clicks or fewer.

Tip: I look at how care provider website careers pages get it wrong and what to do about it in Chapter 7.

What information to collect, when

The online application process itself needs to be carefully thought through. Your goal is to collect *only the minimum* information you require to move the applicant to the next stage. You don't need their entire employment history, their National Insurance number or details of their referees before you have spoken to them. It is much more important to focus on their basic contact information, their right to work, home location and availability, plus ask carefully chosen questions that give you an insight into their motivation to work in care, their personality and workplace behaviour or values. Better yet, you already know their potential because of the channel you used to source them. The classic example here is employee referral, where you have already had a trusted member of staff hand-pick them and vouch for their potential.

Removing barriers

As Mel Kleiman, a leading North American authority on recruiting and selecting hourly paid staff, explains in his excellent book *Hire Tough, Manage Easy*,[16] if you only take phone calls or interview applicants during working hours, you are making it unnecessarily hard for people to apply.

He describes a case where a convenience store advertising for staff only received two responses in three weeks. When it changed its advert to invite people to call its twenty-four-hour recruitment hotline, it received twenty-six qualified responses in just one week. We have repeated exactly this success in social care: one provider launched a twenty-four-hour recruitment hotline and discovered that after the first two months of operating it they had 23% more applications than before.

Also, as Mel points out, if you are only interviewing during working hours, you are making it difficult for the people who are working but looking for a better job to apply and be interviewed. You end up hiring great applicants, not great employees. Certainly, prospective care workers, whom you will be expecting to be available at unsociable times, need to be offered the opportunity to discuss your job or even come to interview at a time to suit them.

Once you've made it easier for people to apply, then consider the next potential roadblock – what sort of welcome do applicants get? How is your phone answered? What about when they visit your office? If an applicant calls out of hours or the recruiter is busy, do staff know to take the caller's details and arrange a time for a call-back? It is critical that all office staff understand the importance of being welcoming to prospective employees, both on the phone and at reception.

When speaking to applicants, actively listen to what they are saying and be (or at least come across as) genuinely interested in why they are considering the role. From my experience, those with emotional maturity will likely have a story of hardship, loss or trauma in their past. Listen respectfully. Most naturally caring people are sensitive to relationships and how others are made to feel. If they don't feel special or sense a connection, they are less likely to turn up at interview.

How applicants hear about the job influences your approach

No two candidates are the same, so find out how they heard about your organisation as this can indicate what their expectations are. For example, if they applied from an internet job board and are currently a paid care worker, then they will most likely want the process to be as quick as possible and to be earning money fast, with a similar shift pattern to what they had before. If, however, you learn that the applicant was told about the role by one of your employees and has no formal paid care experience, then they are much more likely to appreciate a gentle process like an informal chat over a cup of tea to see whether the role could suit them.

You need to sell, but don't oversell

There is much to recommend about a frontline care role to the right person, but it is important that candidates have realistic expectations of the job or they are much more likely to leave early, often during or after induction training. If you do as much as possible to ensure expectations are met, it will have measurable effects on retention. The specific process of communicating extra information about the job to a candidate is called a realistic job preview (RJP), and comes most convincingly from a person currently or previously in that role.

The impact of RJPs on subsequent staff turnover has been measured many times in academic studies since as far back as 1973,[17] and improvements from 9–24% have been attributed to the introduction of an RJP.

Grow your reputation

As care providers, we operate and recruit locally. In the community around our setting, word about us gets around fast amongst applicants, staff, ex-staff and their networks. The smartphones our employees carry mean it is now very easy to leave negative reviews online about an employer, which many prospective applicants will see for months and years to come. These can be on social media, on dedicated employment review sites like Glassdoor, or on internet job boards. Of course, inspection ratings, such as those given by the Care Quality Commission in England, can also be influential.

The importance of protecting your reputation as a good employer has never been more important. Before we look at a few effective ways of marketing your employer brand, I'd like to point out that most of your reputational problems will come from treating staff with disrespect. If you think that is happening in your organisation, then jump straight to Part Three. You need to get that fixed first.

Win some awards

A great way of communicating to applicants that you are a good employer is to win a 'good employer' award and shout about it. Display it on your website, email footers and social media pages. Being a finalist is also fine. If you haven't entered any awards competitions, start now. You'll be surprised how many are run locally and regionally by different groups.

Show you give back to the community

Many applicants looking for a job in the care sector aren't simply looking to work for the most money; they are giving and caring people. So, consider what your organisation and your staff can do to volunteer or support a local charity. If you choose a cause that relates to care or health it can bring you into contact with supporters who could make suitable future staff.

If you are a not-for-profit organisation, then make sure that this is clear and that any fundraisers within your organisation understand the potential of their activity to support your recruitment efforts. Report charitable work on your website, on social media and in newsletters. Don't forget to send the report, together with a high-quality photo, to your local newspaper.

If you are short on time or not sure where to start with getting the word out, then there are communications companies that know social care well.

Ask for feedback as often as you can

Use surveys to measure the satisfaction of both successful and unsuccessful candidates, as well as existing and ex-staff if possible. It can only be a good thing to show that you are interested in improving the experience for these groups. Online tools like Survey Monkey or, my favourite, Typeform, offer questionnaire templates and will host your survey for free. There are also specialist engagement companies that can run these for you.

Tell everyone it is fun to work here

I recommend taking staff out regularly to the pub, for a barbeque or picnics and posting photos on social media. You need to communicate that prospective employees will be joining a family, where it is not all about work.

Try a dog blog

Why not publish a company blog with a twist? A blog helps give your otherwise impersonal organisation a personality and a voice. One very successful homecare business in the United States has a blog 'written' by the company dog (a trained therapy dog and the owner's pet). This gains that workplace great PR all year round and communicates a lot about its culture to applicants. It seems everyone in the care sector in that town has heard of Lucy and her blog.

Dogs have another role in helping you identify suitable staff, as we will see in Chapter 10.

Factor in your setting

Your local setting can strongly influence how you approach your recruitment planning. For example, urban areas will typically have a younger demographic profile than more settled, rural and suburban areas.

Recruiters can often see their recruitment 'territory' as everything within, say, a 6-mile radius (which is the typical commute for social care employees in the UK at least, perhaps not so much the Australian outback) of their location.

However, transport links can mean that when travel time is considered, some areas further away are still within reasonable travel times of their setting or where their clients need care. Conversely, poor transport links or physical barriers such as a river or rail line can mean some journeys take too long, despite being fewer than 6 miles from the workplace. These topographical features can also be psychological barriers to applicants, which will depress the level of interest from prospective staff. Using an out of area dialling code on job adverts can also put off applicants. Fortunately, redirection services are now available to ensure you appear local everywhere in your recruitment territory.

Remap your recruitment hinterland

Take a map of your area and mark out the borders of your recruitment territory using the rule of where you would accept or reject applicants based on their home address alone. Now consider travel times. Using Google Maps or a similar software tool, consider the maximum travel time you think is reasonable for staff in the role.

 Tip: Usually, the more senior the role, the greater distance employees are prepared to travel.

 Tip: Some staff may need to be closer to their work due to other commitments.

 Tip: Remap your territory based on drive time. Has this opened up areas you hadn't previously considered or ruled out those where you currently advertise but have had a poor response?

Look for hotspots

Plot your existing staff's home address postcodes on your territory map. Then look at the distance to your setting or their clients' homes. Can you see patterns or clusters? How far are they typically travelling? Bunches of home addresses indicate potential recruitment hotspots, perhaps as a result of employee referrals – we will explore this in Chapter 9.

Tip: Perhaps there is a local shop that serves these addresses where you can place a postcard advert.

 Tip: Targeted door drops can be effective where there is an indication that the neighbourhood contains the types of people who work for you in a certain role. These work best with a call to action that has a deadline, such as an invite to a recruitment event.

The impact of built-up territory

Think about your area. Would you describe it as city, town/suburban, mainly rural, remote or a mix? The level of urban development and its type will strongly influence what recruitment methods to use. The following is a description of the characteristics of each type of territory and their impact on your recruitment efforts.

City

Characteristics	Which means
Higher ethnicity, more migrants	• 'Within community' word-of-mouth referrals can be powerful
	• Use imagery and language that reflects the audience
	• Community leaders can be influential
	• Higher hours per week on average, but staff don't stay as long
	• Consider language and cultural appreciation support

Characteristics	Which means
High footfall passing your setting	• Consider on-street advertising • How do you handle walk-ins? • How can you encourage these?
Younger population	• Emphasise career pathways or the employability skills they can acquire in the role • A university or nursing course nearby can be a high-quality source of staff
Transient population	• Heavier response to internet job boards, which requires admin effort • Higher staff turnover, so earlier screening will be required

Suburban

Characteristics	Which means
More families	• More interest in flexible working hours • Childcare restrictions could limit availability • May respond to 'return to work' messages
'Grey' households	• Likely to have spare time and fewer restrictions • A desire to give back to the community
Stable, fewer new entrants	• Reputation is more important, as there is a finite population to recruit from

Mainly rural

Characteristics	Which means
Scattered, isolated population	• Many must run a car already • Consider where people gather – community centres, village halls, bus stops, train stations, petrol stations • Although harder to find, rural dwellers are less targeted by other competing forms of employment such as retail or bar work
Reluctant commuters	• Those who commute may respond to 'local work' messages

 Tip: Check out my whiteboard video 'Your Recruitment Hinterland' at www.savingsocialcare.com/videos

Summary

- Recruitment is now a lot about marketing, so sell the job and treat applicants like prospective customers.

- Understand your target applicants' needs and appeal to them with a laser focus.

- Be accessible.

- Build your employer brand in the community around you.

- Remember that your setting will influence the types of likely recruits and their needs.

4

Building An Effective Recruitment System

Is there such a thing as a perfect, one-size-fits-all recruitment process in social care? Unfortunately, not that I have seen. The simple method and structure that makes sense for a single care home accommodating twenty people is not going to work for a national, multi-site homecare provider. It isn't even possible to move your applicants through a single common set of stages in most organisations. Walk-ins and word-of-mouth referrals can skip several steps that online applicants go through, for instance.

But there are shared features of effective recruitment systems that I see time and time again, so it's worth looking at each of those in turn. The most suitable structure for your own needs should then become clear.

Optimised recruitment stages

I am often asked about what recruitment stages would be considered best practice. Of course, there isn't one right way, but if I had to choose, then I would usually have the following steps (the fewer the better):

- Initial application with only the minimum questions required to allow processing to the next stage and an option for applicants just showing interest without the need to provide a CV

- Application review/initial screening (looking for potential, emotional maturity and values, not simply previous paid care experience)

- Outbound telephone call with a script or at least a structure (also listening to how they sound on the phone)

- If successful, book a face-to-face interview date and time as soon as possible

- Follow-up email with information – company/ role, documents to bring, a link to allow the candidate to rebook their interview time and date (if required)

- A reminder prior to interview wishing them 'good luck'

- Face-to-face interview followed by an informal chat with a care worker and a tour, if applicable

- Conditional offer of employment, with a welcome card posted the same day

- Police checks and previous employment and personal references

- Book candidate onto induction training

- Regular communication until they start

The above process can have short-cuts. In a multi-site operation, stages may be divided between a central recruitment or screening team and the local manager. If this is the case, it must be totally clear who is responsible for the next action, with a deadline. More on that shortly.

Of course, the recruitment process itself should not stop at booking the new starter for induction training. I recommend the recruiter account manages the applicant all the way through into at least their first weeks of employment since they have built a relationship by then, as this could help reduce early drop-outs.

Different organisations have different views on how much of the application process should be conducted online. There an efficiency argument for only allowing online applications, but this risks discriminating against, or at least dissuading, certain cohorts of applicants, such as older people or those without access to the internet at home. It's a balance, but my recommendation is to offer a range of options. Make it easy to apply through as many channels as possible, but get the right information early.

There is also a balance in multi-site organisations between what functions a central recruitment team performs and what is left to local managers and administrators. Central recruitment or talent acquisition (TA) teams are usually much more responsive and efficient but it is critical there is a locally led community outreach effort as well as the more volume-led active job seeker-focused approaches favoured by central TA teams.

The counter to that is that local managers can feel they don't have enough say, or can blame a central team for poor-quality or not enough candidates being sent to them. The right choice comes down to specific circumstances, but I favour sending only carefully pre-qualified candidates sourced from internet job boards in particular to busy managers. They quickly lose confidence if a central team's applicants are of poor quality or no-shows.

Responsiveness and accessibility

There is no doubt that responding quickly to an applicant improves your chances of hiring them and enhances your employer brand reputation locally. Especially for online applications, delays longer than twenty-four hours can be interpreted as disinterest, and if you don't make contact within an hour, you risk losing the applicant to competitors. This has never been truer than in the current tight labour market. You might even attract negative comments on social media if you keep people waiting. Offering twenty-four-hour recruitment hotlines, out-of-hours interview slots and keeping applicants informed of the status of their application are best practice techniques that will become increasingly expected.

Many employers still have websites that are not optimised for viewing on a mobile device, despite an increasing percentage of applicants using their phones for their job search and for applying. I will explore this more in Chapter 7.

 Tip: Check your website analytics to see what percentage of visits to your careers page are made from a mobile phone. You may be surprised.

Clear ownership of the recruitment function

A common feature of successful recruitment systems is that there is a clear owner of the process, or a 'champion' as I like to call them. Having someone who wakes up every day thinking about recruitment and moving applicants through the steps toward employment is vital. In my experience, only about 30% of providers have a dedicated recruiter – this is a mistake.

When I see staff shortages, high candidate dropout rates and poor results, the employer often either has no clear ownership of the function or leaves it to a busy manager to pick up between other commitments.

Involvement of frontline care staff

Another feature of high-performing recruitment processes is involvement from people who know what it is like to do the job first-hand. Some of the best recruiters and interviewers I meet have been care workers themselves. They know what the role entails and can convincingly sell the job, as well as manage expectations about some of the challenges. They automatically deliver a realistic job preview. This is why you should aim for employee referral to be your top source of staff.

Tip: Ask a member of your care staff to spend ten minutes with each candidate after their interview with you. The views of frontline care staff on someone who could be the next member of their team are incredibly valuable.

Who makes a good in-house social care recruiter? Let's start by making a clear distinction between what I call a 'high-street recruiter' and the type of recruiter who is successful at sourcing and selecting care workers for their own organisation. From my experience, high-street recruiters struggle to move to an in-house role, especially if this is their first experience of social care.

Professional recruitment consultants are incentivised to place as many candidates as possible. Not all are uninterested in the long-term fit, but they are usually focused on deal flow. In contrast, the in-house recruiter should be measuring their success on how many of their candidates stay at least twelve months. In fact, I would encourage paying your recruiter a bonus linked to this metric.

The best recruiters will be outgoing, upbeat and well-organised communicators. Care experience, even currently caring part-time, helps sell the job, as we will see later. They also need to be resilient. It is a tough job. Make sure they get lots of encouragement and celebrate their successes if you are their boss. Don't have a dedicated recruiter? It's time to change that.

Performance measurement

My starting point for analysing an under-performing recruitment system is to examine specific performance metrics. Having access to accurate data is critical to building a successful recruitment system. If there are key data points missing, you are operating blind, so make it your priority to capture this information.

Here are the common measures I would need to be confidently in control of my recruitment activity. I include some retention statistics too because they are a long-term measure of the success of the recruitment function.

Measure	Questions this helps you answer
List of original sources of applicants	Where are applicants coming from? Note: your website is not an original source. What triggered the applicant to visit it is what you need to know.
	Tip: There is often more than one touchpoint or nudge before they actually apply.
Number of applications by source (and campaign if you changed an important variable such as advert wording)	Are you spending on sources that don't deliver any applicants?
Average time from application to response	Are you responsive enough?

(continued)

Measure	Questions this helps you answer
Cost of each advert or source	How is your budget spent? What is your cost per applicant?
	Tip: Cost per applicant is not as relevant as cost per hire, which in turn is not as relevant as cost per hire at twelve weeks.
Number of applicants by source who are contacted	Which sources have the most genuine applicants?
Number who 'pass' a telephone screen and are booked for interview	What is the quality of this source of applicants?
Percentage who are interviewed and percentage of no-shows by source	What is the quality of this source of applicants?
Average time from application to interview by location	Are you too slow to bring candidates in? Which recruiters are following up well?
Number of interviews by interviewer	Who is seeing the most candidates?
Percentage of offers by interviewer	Who is giving anyone who turns up a job offer?
Percentage of applicants who attend first day of induction training by source and interviewer and location	How are your interviewers performing?
Percentage who complete training by source and interviewer and location	How are your interviewers performing?

(continued)

Percentage who start work by source and interviewer and location	Is your recruitment system under performing?
Reasons for wanting to work in care by source	Are some sources delivering those with a poor motivation?
Percentage of drop-outs by source	Is your recruitment system under performing?
Percentage of drop-outs by reason	Is there anything you can change?
Staff turnover before start date/before training completion/in the first three months/after one year/overall	When are people leaving you?
Reasons for leaving by source and location	Are the causes of leaving controllable?
Full costs of recruiting and training a starter	What is your cost to replace a leaver?
Average hours worked by starter by source in entire employment	What 'tax' are you paying per hour of care delivered for each source?
Sources of staff that stay at least twelve months	What sources should you invest more in?

Cost per hire of each source per successful (stays three months) staff member	True effectiveness cost of recruitment sources
Average time to replace an employee	How long is your recruitment cycle?
Average cost to replace an employee	How much does your staff turnover cost you?

This is not a comprehensive list. The more statistics and data you can collect, the more ability you will have to optimise your recruitment system.

Testing and adjusting

Once you are capturing most of the indicator information above, you are in an excellent position to start testing different aspects of, say, your advert wording or adjusting elements of your system. You may find, for example, that one of your interviewers is performing poorly. Are they offering most or all interviewees a job but suffering a high no-show rate to training or poor three-month retention? Could they be in an operational role and therefore desperate for new staff?

 Tip: Watch my whiteboard video 'The Performance of Interviewers' at www.savingsocialcare.com/videos

Use of technology

Technology has the potential to make life easier for recruiters. Here are a few examples of how.

Applicant tracking systems

Applicant tracking systems (ATS) or candidate management systems are gathering momentum in social care, although they have been widely used in other sectors for many years. ATS is a software application that handles much of the recruitment process. Candidates are directed to the ATS application screens from, say, your website careers page or internet job advert, and so enter their details directly into the ATS recruitment software. This allows recruiters to automate many of the repetitive administrative tasks associated with processing candidates and lets those involved in recruiting and interviewing see a live snapshot of the pipeline and measure performance.

An ATS should give the candidates a better application experience and improve recruitment performance, although in some cases I have seen the ATS application process was too laborious for volume recruitment. There is a new wave of software-as-a-service ATS products coming to market now and these seem to be much more suited to smaller care providers, which make up the majority of the care sector.

At the time of writing there were over 450 different systems available, so choosing the right one for you can be daunting. But I predict most care providers will use an ATS in five years' time, so there's no harm in starting your research now.

Tip: Ask the ATS vendor you are considering for references of other social care employers you can speak to about their experiences. Never commit to an ATS without speaking to a recruiter using it already. I often connect recruiters considering a particular ATS with another who is familiar with that system. In every case, those approached are happy to share their experiences.

Digitised, gamified employee referral schemes

While researching the first edition of *Saving Social Care*, I was struck by the poor delivery rate of paper-based employee referral schemes, despite many care staff saying they loved their job, and they knew people that would also love the job. That resulted in me creating Care Friends, an app that uses behavioural science to maximise the number of care workers who become recruiters. Care Friends has taken off and has generated over 85,000 candidates since it launched in 2020.

Interview appointment booking software

Interview booking is a low value-add and time-consuming aspect of a recruiter's day and can be made easier by technology. Candidates can now choose and book an interview slot to suit themselves online from a list of available options released previously by the interviewing manager. Often, a candidate may agree to an interview time on a call without access to their diary or because they feel under pressure to take what is offered. Allowing them to change a booking when they have had time to consider the available options can improve no-show rates.

With the increase in automated appointment handling for other human service sectors, such as health and wellness, retail banking, financial services, and higher education, candidates will soon expect this convenience.

Online psychometric screening tools

Psychometric screening tools, or tests to assess specific candidate attributes such as personality fit and workplace behaviour, are becoming more widespread in social care recruitment. They can be especially helpful when used early in the process of recruiting large volumes of candidates, helping recruiters prioritise (and eliminate) applicants and providing an objective comparison method as well as targeted probing questions for interview. I will look at these as part of your pre-screening approach in the next chapter.

Desktop texting platforms

Texting (SMS) is by far the best way of communicating with applicants. The average SMS open rate is 97% compared to 18% for email and 90% of text messages are read within three minutes.[18] Responding can just require a single sentence.

Consider using a desktop online platform to make it easy to text at scale rather than relying on your phone.

Summary

- Candidates like simplicity, speed and not having to duplicate information.

- Measure whatever you can, as without data, it is impossible to refine and improve.

- Try applying for a job yourself – how easy was it? How fast was the response? Was the recruiter friendly? Did they ask the right questions?

5
Pre-screening And Values-based Recruitment

Being able to both reach and identify high-potential applicants and those who are best avoided early on is a critical part of volume recruiting in any sector. Obviously, you owe it to those you care for to take necessary steps to select only suitable staff. But we need to go well beyond that and prioritise sourcing those with the values we seek. The costs of hiring mistakes can have a major and long-term impact on a care provider, as we will see in Chapter 12.

Pre-screening and recruiting for values matters

The further you allow unsuitable applicants to get through your recruitment and training process, the more they cost you in time, effort and money. They will likely have low job attachment, leave early and so incur the cost of re-recruitment. Existing staff will be carefully watching who you consider good enough to work alongside them – 'they just hire anyone these days' is not what you want them to think.

Pre-screening is the process of identifying extra information from an applicant at an early stage in the recruitment process. This helps to inform you of which people to prioritise from your pool of applicants as well as guiding an interviewer on what issues to probe further. It also minimises those costs and the risks to your business from miss-hiring.

As you will discover throughout this book, recruiting only those with the right values for a direct care role is at the heart of building a loyal, high-performing workforce. **Values-based recruitment (VBR)** can be introduced ahead of pre-screening. As an example, I've found that employee referrals are ten to fifteen times more likely to convert to a loyal care worker than those from internet job boards. This is because they have been selected by your current employee based on their values.

However, recruiters can often feel under pressure to take on applicants they have reservations about because of a shortage of staff. Some managers over-rely on a face-to-face interview for selection, despite this method alone being only about 8% better than pure chance in selecting suitable staff.[19]

There is a move toward simplifying the candidate experience and making it slick and easy, of which I am a proponent. Adding pre-screening steps while asking a little more of an applicant does not have the same off-putting effect as a laborious and frustrating application process. Pre-screening hurdles are important, not only for the information they collect, but because they dissuade the indifferent and timewasters as well as testing to see if applicants can follow basic instructions in a timely manner.

In all the research I have undertaken, I have discovered that a common characteristic of the best care providers is that they emphasise their pre-screening process as a core part of maintaining the best workforce. Let's see what tools and methods they use and what they are screening for.

The basics

Prioritise high-conversion sources

As the labour market tightens up, it becomes more important to prioritise high-quality sources, not only because there are fewer candidates out there, but retention rates tell us that it is futile to 'fill the training course' in social care. As it isn't realistic to rely solely on these sources, pre-screening provides an important early filter.

How did applicants hear of your organisation?

The source the applicant applied from can be an accurate indicator of their likely suitability. From my extensive research with recruiters, backed up by similar studies in the United States by Stephen Tweed and others,[20] I have found there is a common pattern in the volume and quality of applicants from the typical recruitment sources used by most care employers.

The highest quality candidates come from sources connected to your organisation (such as referrals or returners), while the poorest quality come from sources where the primary motivation is a focus on finding paid employment of any kind (such as job centres and internet job boards). I will look at this in detail in Part Two.

Triaging

There are some basic pieces of personal information that every applicant expects to provide when they apply for a job, such as name, address and contact details along with their employment status. If this information is in the form of a CV or on your application form, then you can easily see if it contains spelling mistakes or poor grammar. If you are collecting this information over the phone, listen to the applicant's tone of voice. Is it friendly? Do they speak clearly and sound eager and helpful?

'Killer questions'

After these basics, every recruiter will have a set of mandatory requirements before processing the applicant. These are often referred to as 'killer questions' and include categories like an applicant's right to work in the country, their ability to understand and speak English to a required standard, their salary expectations, whether they live locally, their access to suitable transport, their availability and willingness to work unsocial hours. These are covered either on the application form or asked in a phone call.

Frustratingly, the answers you receive to these questions are not always honest. Most recruiters will have regular cases where an applicant has said they are available to work unsocial hours until they've completed their training, and then suddenly they announce restricted hours of availability. However, it is possible to detect a lack of openness by listening to how the applicant answers your question. Do they sound evasive or non-committal? Are they giving a qualified answer, such as 'probably'?

Follow up a positive response to the question 'Can you work alternate weekends?' with a clarification question like 'Is there anything that could prevent you from regularly working those hours?' This might flag up commitments that make it impossible for an applicant to meet that claim.

Salary expectations

If you have displayed a pay rate on your job advert, it can be easy to assume that the applicant has noted and is fine with it by virtue of the fact they've submitted their application, only to discover later that they drop out at interview or offer stage because the salary is not what they expected.

A good pre-screening question is to ask the open question 'Can you remind me of your salary requirements?' You might be surprised by the answer. If a candidate was earning significantly more in their previous role then it is well worth clarifying that they are comfortable making a commitment to your company despite the pay rate being lower. This is a motivation question, and we'll look at that topic in more detail now.

Motivation

If I could only ask one pre-screening question, it would be to probe why the applicant wants to work in care if they are not already a care worker. If they are an existing paid care worker, I'd want to find out what is motivating them to apply to me. As we saw in Chapter 2, research undertaken by Northwestern University in Chicago demonstrated a powerful link between the motivation of the worker and the outcomes of the consumers they care for.[21] Care worker skills can be taught, but the right motivation is paramount. Is this 'just a job' to them or more of a calling?

Commute time

How far applicants must travel to their new workplace, or the locations of their consumers' homes, can play a major role in how long they stay, or even if they can be bothered to come to the interview you have booked with them. The average commute in the UK is 5.9 miles for a care worker in a residential home outside London,[22] and IQ Timecard tells us the average distance from a homecare worker's home to their first call is 4.5 miles.[23] Interviews at your office may be unnecessarily dissuading homecare candidates from far flung parts of your territory as their work would be based near their homes. Meet more locally to where their work is, or at the setting they will be working in.

 Tip: Watch my whiteboard video 'Your Recruitment Hinterland' at www.savingsocialcare.com/videos

Psychometric screening

Behavioural assessments are not new. In fact, they have been in widespread use for workplace selection since the 1950s. The factors that held back the use of psychometrics in social care until recent years included high cost-per-test fees, questions that were inaccessible to the education level of many applicants, poor English skills and too much effort required on the part of managers to interpret the results. All those issues have now been overcome and we are seeing a steady growth in the adoption of some form of behavioural screening by care employers.

A psychometric assessment is a consistent and fair method of discovering hidden risks. If used in combination with other screening techniques, it should improve hiring decisions and reduce workplace risks. The results reported from care providers using such software show a measurable reduction in disciplinary issues amongst the workforce and improvements in staff turnover.

Psychometric tools can assess personality fit with a job role, workplace behaviours, or seek to understand a candidate's values. Details that would be unlikely to be discovered in an interview can be quickly evaluated using an online questionnaire completed in the candidate's own time. Good psychometric reports then suggest probing questions for use in a face-to-face interview, based on identified risks or personality mismatches with a frontline care role.

CASE STUDY: Using Screening Tests at Franciscan Health System

One of the earliest independent evaluations of workplace psychometric testing in social care was undertaken at two large nursing homes as part of the Franciscan Health System of Dayton (FHSD) in Ohio in 1990.

FHSD had an annual turnover of nursing assistants of 146%, with most leaving within the first six months of employment. Those who did stay weren't doing a good job. The main reasons for staff leaving were job dissatisfaction, poor performance and absenteeism. Such high staff turnover was also affecting the quality of care and putting more pressure on existing staff.

The HR team introduced three assessments to provide an objective, validated way of identifying the right candidates and to overcome selection based on the managers' gut feelings. After selection testing was implemented in mid-1990, nurse assistant turnover rates dropped suddenly and continued to fall. Previously, an average of forty-six frontline staff had been dismissed each year. After the psychometric tests were implemented, only seven were terminated in the ten-month period measured. The overall annualised staff turnover was measured to have dropped to less than 27%.

FHSD found the new selection method helped them identify and remove applicants who only wanted a job and focus on those who genuinely wanted to work in frontline care. HR staff found that new starters who scored well on the tests settled into their care facility faster and were more cooperative than those hired under the old method.[24]

With the increased competition for workers, it is important to ensure that introducing a psychometric test does not dissuade candidates. Tests should take no longer than a few minutes.

Situational judgement testing

Although not widely used by social care employers, situational judgement tests (SJTs), are good tests of common sense and on-the-job problem-solving. These can use a written, verbal or video-based scenario describing a typical problem that a frontline care worker might face. Usually, there is a choice of answers.

Group assessments

These can be an effective way of evaluating many candidates in one go and get good feedback from the employers who run them, although most employers are continually recruiting and group sessions are usually only run periodically, which means there is a risk of candidates dropping out while they wait. The assessments can help recruiters see how each person works as part of a team and how they perform under pressure. They are most suitable for bulk recruitment ahead of the launch of a new care service, where large numbers of candidates need to be evaluated at the same time.

Summary

- Values-based recruitment is recommended as the basis for your recruitment strategy.

- Robust pre-employment screening can ensure the protection of vulnerable consumers and reduce staff turnover and wasted cost and effort.

- Several pre-screening techniques are widely used or gaining popularity, such as telephone screening and psychometric testing.

- Recruiters can be more confident of the likely potential of an applicant by learning how they heard about the company, considering any existing connection and probing their reasons for wanting to work in a frontline care role.

6
Upgrading The Interview

Face-to-face interviews are usually the primary method of final selection of care workers. Having said that, I have come across a case where applicants were not interviewed at all, but invited straight to induction training after a brief phone call (yes, really). Mostly, though, the interview has a big, though perhaps overstated, influence on what decision is made.

An imperfect selection tool

In my view, the interview is a flawed selection method in social care, especially if it is over-relied upon as the main criterion for making a job offer. Psychologists agree, measuring the predictive accuracy of an unstructured interview at 0.3 (where 1.0 is perfect prediction).[25] On the plus side (let's start positively), many interviewers I meet in social care are seasoned sector managers or recruiters with a clear idea of what they are looking for. So, I think the odds for them are reduced as they are looking out for values more than what is written on the application form.

Without playing to the gallery, I think female interviewers have the edge on men (certainly on me) at interviewing. They seem to have an extra sense, some other-worldly awareness of 'hire-me-at-your-peril' signs that is not available to those of us with a Y chromosome. However, there's a lot pitched against relying on this technique.

The interview environment is not reflective of care work. Often, the candidates with the polished answers are simply well-practised, doing the rounds of interviewing. Conversely, a parent returning to work, who perhaps has low self-esteem and is shy and sensitive, may come across poorly in a formal interview.

Interviewers can suffer from bias, of course, being over-reliant on first impressions, and they may feel under pressure to hire due to workforce shortages. We know that the high rate of no-shows in the sector (in my experience, 40–60%) can make the candidate who does show up appear more suitable than they are.

 Tip: Check out my whiteboard video 'The Performance of Interviewers' at www.savingsocialcare.com/videos

Improving no-shows

No-shows to interviews are disruptive and frustrating. With often fewer than 50% of interviewees appearing, and not all of those arriving with the correct documentation at the right time, this is an endemic problem. As the labour market has tightened up, so candidate behaviour has worsened. There is a lot of choice for job seekers now – and they know it. But there is a lot you can do to improve the turn-up rate.

Here are eight tips that I have tested that each nudged up the ratio of interviewees who appear.

1. **Changing your recruitment source.** There is a clear correlation between the source of the candidate and whether they show up. The worst offenders are those from internet job boards and the job centre; the best are usually word-of-mouth referrals.

2. **Respond quickly and remind.** Communication and responsiveness are so important in today's

recruitment market. Once an interview has been booked, most recruiters will follow up with a confirmation email. The better ones will call or text and remind the candidate as the date approaches. Software can help with automated reminders via text message.

3. **Out-of-hours options.** Not all candidates can make a 9am–5pm interview slot. We know from US research that about 19% of care workers in a residential home have a second job, as do 31% of those who work in the community.[26] I haven't yet found comparable UK data, but it is probably not dissimilar. For an applicant to attend your interview can mean them losing earnings or having to phone in sick to their current employer, which makes good employees feel bad. Consider interviewing early or late, or even at weekends. In my experience, the best time is late afternoon or early evening.

4. **Check the distance from the applicant's home.** Care workers don't like commuting. The average distance from home to work for a residential homecare worker is 6 miles; for homecare to their first call, 4.5 miles.[27] If your candidate is much farther away than this from your care home or first homecare client, they might well think twice about bothering to come along for the interview. Check how far away they are and call back the outliers to double-check their intentions. Should you meet them locally or choose a video interview format?

5. **Ask them to do something that requires a little effort.** When the application processes were amended to include a short personality questionnaire, researchers found that those who followed the instructions and submitted their results appeared for interview nine times out of ten compared to four times out of ten for a control group.[28] Interviewers were much more able to predict who would attend interviews based on this action alone. So, consider asking candidates to do something in preparation for their interview as a test of their commitment. For the best results, it should be of interest and value to them in some way.

6. **Have they heard of you?** Candidates are less likely to show up if they have never heard of your organisation. If you have spent time building your employer brand in the community or they have an existing connection, they will feel more confident about working for you and are more likely to show up. In research undertaken by a care jobs website in the US, a third of applicants said they were less likely to show up if they had not heard of the employer.[29] In a fragmented market like ours, there are hardly any nationally known brands but what matters most is awareness and reputation locally. This is not expensive to achieve.

7. **Is video interviewing as effective as face to face?** The pandemic forced us to move to video-based interviewing. Most have since returned to face to face, as it allows the interviewer to

much better evaluate body language and other non-verbal cues. There is still a role for video interviewing, especially where a face-to-face interview would add a lengthy delay, or you have candidates from high-quality sources.

8. **Go as high touch as you can.** Increasing the number of connections with a candidate prior to face-to-face interview can really improve no-shows. Cohesion, specialists in social care recruitment solutions, achieves 70% turn-up rates[30] by emphasising timely communication and explicitly asking for commitment at the telephone interview stage.

Pre-interview checks

Assuming the candidate actually arrives for the interview, you can learn quite a lot about them before you ask a single question. First, are they on time? If they aren't, did they phone and explain why they would be late? It does not bode well for their employment with you if they start by missing their appointment.

If they have arrived by car, it is worth a member of staff taking a look in the car park. There is a story from a US homecare provider of a member of staff doing just that and seeing a car full of people, including the candidate, smoking drugs prior to the interview. As a minimum, ask whoever greets the interviewee how they were treated by the applicant.

A clever tip suggested by Leigh Davis, a leading US expert on homecare candidate screening and interviewing, is what he calls the Box Test.[31] This involves arranging the chairs where candidates wait to be called for interview near a closed door. When the candidate has settled in and is probably looking at their phone, a member of staff picks up an empty bankers' box (a cardboard storage container) as if it is heavy and walks towards the closed door with both hands full. Does the candidate leap up with a smile and open the door, or do they ignore the struggling soon-to-be colleague? This is a great test of courtesy and awareness of others before even asking an interview question.

We've mentioned studying interactions between the interviewee and their prospective colleagues, but what about those they are seeking to care for or support? Many providers who have consumers on site can see how the candidate interacts with them as part of their visit. This can reveal much more than the interview itself and is respectful to those who will be interacting with the prospective care worker regularly.

Putting candidates at ease

An interview is almost always stressful for the interviewee, but sometimes for the interviewer too, especially if they are new to it or lack training or support. Best practice suggests making the interview room less threatening by avoiding having a desk between the interviewer and the candidate. If possible, comfortable chairs can help bring informality and relax everyone. It is also important to ensure the interviewer is prepared and isn't under pressure or distracted by interruptions.

With the tightening of the labour market, an interview is as much about a candidate evaluating your organisation as it is about you assessing them. But often interviewers treat the interview as a one-way process where the candidate has to prove they are worth employing. Most good candidates already have several offers, or they soon will do if other care providers discover them, so it is important to make your case for why they should want your job and why your organisation is different, as we discussed in Chapter 3.

With frontline care roles, though, we need a balance. Airbrushing out the unpleasant aspects of personal care might help fill places on your induction course, but expect a high dropout rate once new starters discover this part of the job. On the other hand, full disclosure before relationships with consumers have been formed can put off promising candidates unnecessarily. Build the relationship first. If you have recruited for values, you should be able to confidently discuss the challenges of the role. This can be most convincing when delivered by someone who is, or has recently been, in the role.

Selling the job – and being realistic about what it entails – is best done by a member of your care team, who generally like to have a say in who will potentially be joining them. This sends out several important messages to the candidate that you are:

- Not hiding the true working conditions

- A boss who respects your staff and values their opinions

- Signifying their importance as a future employee

What this does is improve the likelihood of the candidate choosing your offer over others. Of course, if you have sourced the candidate from an employee referral, this will have already happened.

The interviewee's urge to exaggerate

Lying or exaggerating in a job interview is commonplace, and more likely with those who really need a job. Because care work requires few formal qualifications, it can attract people whose goal is to make some money while they continue to look for better paid work elsewhere. One of an interviewer's challenges is deciding if they are getting truthful answers to their questions.

Mel Kleiman[32] recommends telling the interviewee exactly what you expect with the following opening question, which has proved highly effective at reducing incidences of lying:

> 'I'm going to be very open and truthful with you about the job and our company and I hope you're going to be open and honest with me about yourself. It doesn't matter if you've ever resigned, or had difficulty with a former boss. As long as you tell me we can take it under consideration. But, if you don't tell me and we find a problem when we do our background checks and look into your history, I can't hire you. Do you understand what it is I want?'
>
> — Reproduced courtesy of Humetrics Press

There is much research into the physical signs of candidate unsuitability, including a lack of honesty, such as certain kinds of body language, eye contact, tone of voice and so on.

Interview questions

I am often asked for suitable interview questions, or to review a set of questions currently in use. In many cases, interviewers aren't sure why they are asking the questions on the sheet in front of them – or what constitutes a 'right' answer. Questions can be chopped and changed and not reviewed for several years, so take a fresh look at what you ask. Broadly speaking, there are four varieties of questions I come across most in social care recruitment.

Leading or skills-based questions

These will give you very little indication of a candidate's suitability for the job. Care work competences, such as correct moving and handling, will be taught anyway. It is the underlying motivation and suitability for the role you want to get to.

Examples of this type of leading question are:

- What do you like most about care work?

- Why would you be good as a care worker?

These do not get to the heart of a candidate's suitability for a care role and are of limited value, especially for those who have not already held a paid care role.

Situational questions

These focus on the future and seek to identify problem-solving skills, commonsense and the ability or expertise of the candidate to do the job. They often begin with 'What would you do if...?' For example, 'Imagine you discovered a client lying on the floor in distress. What would you do first and why?'

Because these are theoretical, they may never have happened to the candidate before, so it can be easy for them to impress, particularly if they have some prior knowledge of the questions you will likely ask. I hear of cases where candidate placement agencies 'apply' first for the job so they can access the questions to coach their candidates.

Behavioural questions

These seek to establish, from specific examples of past workplace behaviour, how suitable a candidate will be for this job. By using responses provided by the candidate, it is possible, with probing, to confirm the truth and have confidence that the response will be indicative of their likely behaviour in your employment.

An example of a behavioural question would be, 'Tell me about a time when you had to deal with someone who was very unhappy. What was the situation and how did you handle it?'

This type of questioning is effective at proving a candidate's actual workplace behaviour and is popular with social care interviewers. The tailored questions provided by an applicant's psychometric assessment usually follow this format to probe a specific weakness, based on their responses.

Values-based interviewing

There is a move toward VBA (values, behaviours and attitudes interviewing) in social care in the UK, pioneered by leading practitioners like Kerry Cleary of VBA Consulting,[33] Oxfordshire County Council, as well as Skills for Care, the strategic body for workforce development in adult social care in England.[34]

VBA questions are closely aligned to behavioural questions, but go further by focusing on why an applicant made those choices in the workplace – effectively understanding their values. Once these values have been identified, they can be compared to the values of the organisation.

A typical VBA starter question, such as this one from Kerry Cleary, might be, 'Tell me about a time when a client or customer was rude or aggressive toward you?'

Follow-up questions would then be:

- What did you do?

- What would you have liked to have done if you could?

- What was the outcome?

- Why do you think it was important to take action in this situation?

- What would you do if you were in a similar situation in our organisation?

- What would you do if someone was behaving aggressively toward one of our consumers?

Values-based interviewing requires commitment and should be delivered by two trained interviewers. This can make it a challenge for a busy, understaffed care office, but it's worth making the investment in it. VBA interviews often take a little longer than a typical social care interview, but research indicates improvements in recruiting high-performing and effective staff if this approach is followed.

If you are based in the UK, Skills for Care and a number of local authorities offer training in VBA interviewing for social care.

At the end of the interview

Ask the candidate if they have any questions, which can be illuminating. If they don't seem interested or their questions focus on money or benefits then that should sound warning bells, but it is important to let them cover any unanswered queries. Many interviewers will make a verbal offer then and there, and with the competition for candidates, this is increasingly the case. But it is best to reflect on the candidate and review all the other information you have, including asking your colleagues how the candidate interacted with them prior to the interview.

Once an employment offer is made and accepted, then the candidate becomes a new starter and your focus turns to avoiding them dropping out during the 'on-boarding' period – the time from accepted offer to completion of training and shadowing. We are going to look at that in Part Three.

Past employment references

Taking up past employment references can take time, but the bigger challenge is learning anything valuable from them, since most employers are reluctant to disclose negative information that may be challenged by the employee. Make a phone call to the new starter's line manager to see if you can learn any more.

The question that previous employers are most willing to answer is, 'Would you re-hire this person?' This can be considered more of a company policy position rather than a personal view that could get an individual into hot water. Finally, time the pause between you asking and them answering. That can be very telling.

Summary

- Your no-show rate will decrease as your recruitment sources improve.

- Beware – the candidates with the best answers at interview can be job hoppers or coached.

- Use pre-interview checks to augment your face-to-face judgement.

- Don't forget to let candidates know why they should want to work for you.

PART TWO
SOURCING CREATIVELY

'The most frequently used techniques are not the
most effective, and the most effective techniques
are not used by many.'
   — Stephen Tweed

7
Finding Applicants Online

Online recruitment appeals to busy recruiters as, particularly on internet job boards, it involves little upfront effort to place an advert, can be free (although this is increasingly rare) and managed from the convenience of your desk. However, there are major disadvantages to over-relying on this channel to find quality staff.

The options for online recruitment are many and growing. I will focus on the five most common ones: internet job boards, social media, your company website, CV Search and pay-per- click/Google Ads.

 Tip: Watch my video 'The Impact of Recruitment Sources' at www.savingsocialcare.com/videos

Internet job boards

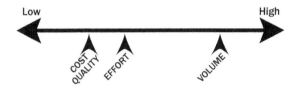

Internet job boards are usually good for delivering applicant volume (although this seems to be declining), but weaker at delivering a consistent quality of frontline care candidates.

As a guide, based on feedback from care providers who use them, between 1–4% of internet job board care worker applicants will make it to employment with you, and typically fewer than 1% of those original applicants will last twelve months in a frontline care role[35] if robust pre-screening is not in place. There is no doubt care employers over-rely on this channel and have seen an increase in interview no-shows, a drop in staff retention and a decline in care quality as a result.

Given the disadvantages, I strongly recommended that internet job boards are not the main recruitment channel you use. However, they remain an important source of applicants, so how do you optimise your recruitment activity using this source?

How to succeed on internet job boards

There are six elements to consider when seeking to improve your internet job board performance.

1. **Pay rate.** Job seekers on internet job boards can be motivated by money, and the standardised format of adverts means that your rate of pay is one of the few differentiators between you and other employers. It's also a major factor in the number of applications you'll receive.

   Research has shown that offering a salary range rather than a single pay rate is the most effective method to drive applications, although showing one pay rate is an improvement on not declaring one. If you are paying above the local market rate this should improve responses, although government mandated pay floors, such as the National Living Wage in the UK, have significantly reduced opportunities to differentiate using pay alone.

2. **Ad visibility.** If you are placing free job adverts, you must be prepared to refresh them regularly to keep them high in the applicants' search results. Best practice tells us that using many localised adverts and ensuring they are newly posted for the peak job search window of Monday to Wednesday will maximise your ad visibility.

3. **Make your headline stand out.** Most social care recruiters use the same format for job ad headlines, such as job title, often a pay rate, and possibly 'urgently required', resulting in no stand out. Testing in the US care sector has demonstrated that headlines asking a question about the job seeker such as 'Could you be one of our best care workers?' or 'Are you our next care worker?' can deliver a better quality of applicant and could increase responses against a backdrop of similar headlines.[36] This is because people like being asked about themselves, so these headlines stand out. Being different can help attract attention, but remember that most job boards are search engines too, so use a job title that people will be searching for to maximise hits.

4. **Advertisement copy.** Attention spans, particularly of online job seekers, are generally short, so it is important to sell the job and the organisation immediately rather than start with a list of restrictions or requirements that can appear unfriendly.

5. **Strong call to action.** Some social care recruiters in the US ask internet job board applicants to phone in person to apply rather than simply attaching a CV to an email application. There is ongoing research into the benefits of asking applicants to make some kind of effort versus clicking on multiple adverts without much thought. This also tests their ability to follow simple instructions.

6. **Responsiveness.** Job board applicants may well have applied to multiple adverts and, given the tightening recruitment market, it is important to respond quickly, perhaps outside of office hours, to engage applicants before other employers do.

It is surprising to me that the return on investment with internet job board spend rarely seems to be measured. I would ask readers to gauge the success of any of their sources not by how many applications fill their inboxes each day, but by how many of these applicants become successful and loyal employees, and how much was invested in recruitment and training, including in those who left prematurely. The number of applicants you receive is not the measure to base recruitment success on.

In summary, though, internet job boards remain an important source of care staff with some success stories. However, it is critical not to create a dependency on this method alone, and to be aware of the quality and tenure of the new starters sourced this way compared to other options.

Pros:

- High reach amongst active job seekers

- Easy for applicants to apply

- Convenient for advertisers to place adverts

Cons:

- Highly competitive

- Requires huge screening effort

- Can be expensive and is always wasteful

- Only reaches those actively looking for work –
  a shrinking group

 Tip: Watch my whiteboard video on the impact of recruitment sources at www.savingsocialcare.com / videos

Social media

Feedback from employers suggests that applicants
sourced from social media are overall of a better quality than those from internet job boards. Given that
there is an element of referral and personal connection on social media, and much less competition from
other employers, this would make sense.

The major player, at least so far, is still Facebook, which
we will concentrate on here, but I am hearing reports of
sporadic successes on other platforms such as TikTok,
Instagram and NextDoor. Contrary to expectations,

Facebook's demographic profile is not simply Millennial-focused. In fact, its popularity amongst older users is growing, and it has a female bias (in January 2023 54% of Facebook users were female compared to 46% male).[37] As mums and dads start using Facebook, so their teenage children decide it is no longer cool and move on to other platforms, so there is a better demographic spread than you might think.

There are several options open to employers who want to advertise, share job openings and build their employer brand using Facebook:

- Posting job adverts on your organisation's Facebook page so staff and others may like and share them

- Posting job adverts or good employer branding posts on local job pages or community or group pages

- Targeted paid advertising with sponsored posts or 'boosting'

Targeted advertising on Facebook can be directed to a user's gender, age, interests, location and even workplace. Obviously, the more filters you apply, the less the reach. Spend can also be capped to a specific budget.

So far, results for social care recruitment have been hit and miss. Decisions over the timing, imagery, wording, targeting and call to action can dramatically affect results. I could fill the rest of this book with a 'How To' guide on Facebook recruitment advertising, but since there are lots of online resources – including Facebook itself, of course – and specialist social media agencies who can do that much better, I have just covered the basics here.

Before you start using Facebook to generate job applicants there are several things to get right. First, you'll need a business Facebook page. It is also important to ensure your company website's careers page is mobile-enabled as this is the most popular viewing platform for care staff. Your application process needs to be streamlined to allow respondents to register interest quickly, whether within Facebook (preferred) or via the website link you offer.

Create an attention-grabbing advert or post. The key word here is engagement. You only have a few moments to get a viewer's attention, so choosing an image (or even better, a video) that shows candidates why they would want to work for you and in social care is critical.

Don't forget you are up against cats playing pianos. Facebook is a social rather than 'professional' platform like LinkedIn, so an element of humour or quirkiness can work well, as long as you don't compromise your brand values. The title and wording you use is also important. Asking a question works well to engage viewers.

Choose a call to action. The most direct call to action is to encourage viewers to click through to your website careers page, but make sure it is super simple to register interest. For example, you can set up a 'basic message complete' section on Facebook that just asks for name and number. Not every post has to be a direct request for applicants; many companies mix up their posts to include celebrating the success of their employees or highlighting charitable work or company activities. These can be shared by staff with their Facebook networks.

Be tenacious when following up. Sector media specialists Social Media 92 report an average of eight to ten outbound contact attempts by phone, text and email to get an initial response from those showing interest in a job posting on Facebook or Instagram.[38] Are you giving up too soon?

Other platforms. The jury is still out on how effective other social media channels, such as Instagram, TikTok and NextDoor, will become for recruiting. TikTok's short-form video format is popular with a young demographic, as Facebook's users age, but you'll likely need some expert help to manage multiple platforms effectively.

Be cautious about posting urgent pleas for staff – it sends the wrong message and cannot be repeated regularly.

A social media presence for your employer brand opens up the possibility of negative comments, of course, and active management is required. Recruiters have found that curating their recruitment activity on social media takes up a surprising amount of time, so it is important to record the time and cost you put in for the return you get. Testing is also important since it is easy to get just one element wrong. Perseverance usually pays off.

Pros:

- High reach and tight targeting

- Element of referral and personal connection

- Range of advertising options

- Less competition than cluttered internet job boards

- Builds your local employer brand

Cons:

- Requires trial and error or professional guidance from a digital agency

- Can take a lot of time to manage and be distracting

- Requires persistence to get a contact

- Early days for social care recruitment and limited best practice is available

Your company website

Placing job adverts on your own organisation's website is commonplace, but its effectiveness can be highly variable. Unless you are a known 'brand' then you will need to make efforts to drive job seeker traffic to it, either from a job board, search engine optimisation, partner websites, social media or a paid method such as Google Ads.

I strongly recommend testing how easy it is for an applicant to apply or register their interest in your vacancies. In a surprising number of cases when I test-apply on providers' websites, I discover the process requires many clicks or taps simply to reach the application page. While it is important not to make it too easy to apply without any consideration or commitment, equally avoid an overlong or frustrating application process.

We looked at optimising what I call the 'candidate journey' in detail in Chapter 4.

How website careers pages get it wrong

Most care providers' website careers sections could do better. Here are my top six gripes and how to fix them.

1. **Don't use stock shots.** Whoever took the photo of a blonde twenty-year-old nurse-type care worker with perfect teeth holding the hand of an adoring grandmother must have retired long ago on the royalties from care providers. Stock shots create less reassurance amongst prospective employees, not more. It is obvious that it isn't a real employee. Use images of your care workers and clients (with permission, of course). They are much more believable.

2. **No social proof.** If there is no voice of the current staff, then applicants will wonder why. Use real attributed quotes and short video clips. I especially recommend a selection of video clips of real staff talking to camera. Include your key target candidate profiles that we identified earlier. Prospective applicants like to see whom they will work with. This builds bonds and

makes it more likely they will go on to submit an application.

3. **No fun.** Okay, social care isn't quite the same as working at Disney, but try to convey your organisation's personality and show staff having fun and smiling. Never forget that candidates have a choice.

4. **No mobile optimisation.** An increasing number of hits on your careers pages will be from a mobile phone. Your website is already mobile optimised, right?

5. **Not giving candidates clear reasons to join your company.** This is a common mistake – not actually listing why they would want to work for you. Have a 'Ten reasons to work here' list. Can't think of ten? Ask your staff.

6. **No signposting.** What happens next? What are the steps to apply? What can applicants expect? How long will it take? What are you looking for? These questions don't get answered often enough.

One of the challenges of applications from your own website is understanding what original source drove the applicants to apply via your site. The most common driver of traffic is a job board, so the quality is rarely better, although there is some evidence that those who have taken time to research your organisation are more likely to turn up to an interview.

Pros:

- Ownership of the 'sales pitch'

- Video and valuable content about the role and organisation

- A vital 'landing page' for all other online or offline recruitment advertising

Cons:

- Often hides the original source of the applicant

- Very limited traffic unless job seekers are aware of the organisation some other way

- Managing vacancies and keeping content fresh on a website can be an effort, particularly for smaller employers

CV search

CV search offers employers the opportunity to be notified of recently updated CVs that match their search criteria. Several job boards and specialist websites offer this facility, and the employer pays when they contact the job seeker. This method has been used particularly to target those employed in the same role as an employer is hiring for, and search terms invariably use the word 'care', although it involves a lot of outbound telephone work. There is wastage, making this method quite expensive and time-consuming.

 Tip: A side benefit of regularly using CV search is that you may identify those from your own workforce who are thinking of leaving, which could allow you to address issues before that happens.

Pros:

- Targets those thinking of a move

- Only pay to contact

- Can be effective when seeking qualified staff currently in a similar role

Cons:

- Requires effort and telephone work

- Response rates can be poor as it includes those not actively looking

- Candidates will probably also be approached by competitors

Google Ads

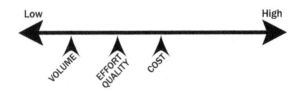

Google Ads is a powerful advertising medium. It allows a care provider to advertise to a highly targeted audience on the Google search engine. When a prospective candidate in your local area searches using any number of words or phrases you have selected, then your advert, with a web link, appears on their results page. You only pay for the advert when someone clicks on it and visits your website (or, more likely, a specific landing page you have created for this purpose). The price you pay varies mainly by how much demand there is for the same keywords from other advertisers.

Although Google Ads can be successful for many businesses, it seems to be weaker for the recruitment of care workers. Most providers that I am aware of who have tried Google Ads for this purpose have been supported by a digital agency that markets this service to small businesses. That means there is a management fee and potentially a term commitment, but it should come with specialist expertise.

Unless you or someone in your organisation is a Google Ads expert, then attempting to test and run campaigns alone can be a considerable time commitment, and you are likely to waste money as you take time to learn what works best. But even with professional help, more providers have reported a poor return than that they've become fans. What isn't yet clear is if the agency fees and input are at fault or Google Ads itself. There is also little data on the quality and tenure of new starters recruited from this source.

Pros:

- Target geographically to minimise wastage

- Increases brand awareness

- Budget can be capped

- High audience reach

Cons:

- Doesn't seem to deliver meaningful conversions in many cases

- Campaigns may need six- to twelve-month commitments

- Click-through conversion rates can be low

- It's a challenge to balance targeting with broad appeal

- Easy to waste large sums of money in the optimisation phase

Summary

- Make online sources of candidates a core part of your recruitment plan, but don't over-rely on job boards.

- Make sure your website application process is clear and simple.

- Advertising on Facebook and other social media channels could be a big opportunity to reach out to suitable candidates in the community around you.

- Google Ads should be an effective method of finding staff with a much wider reach than job boards, but I haven't yet identified many examples of success.

8
Traditional Media

By traditional media, I mean print and radio. Print is a declining or obsolete medium for many care employers, mainly due to the collapse of the local newspaper classified or display advertising market since 2000. (The price didn't collapse, of course, only the readership). However, printed adverts can exist in many formats and this channel shouldn't be ruled out too quickly.

Generally, printed adverts don't perform as well as more active recruitment methods such as face-to-face contact with targeted community groups or video, but they can offer both reach and targeting. Radio is not so commonly used by care providers and doesn't have a good track record of results. We'll review it at the end of this section.

Local newspapers

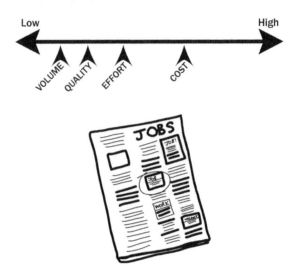

With a much-reduced readership for situations vacant sections and high advertising costs, care providers don't usually speak enthusiastically about the results they get from placing job adverts in the local press. Although each publication will have varying reach and readership, you might expect to receive from zero to a handful of applications from an advert costing several hundred pounds. This might yield a single new starter, or maybe none, and so the cost of acquiring that employee can be much higher than alternatives.

However, local newspapers tend to have an older readership and could be read by those in the community who would not be reached using other sources, such as internet job boards. There is also less competition from other providers since most have moved online. An occasional advert might yield results, but increasingly local newspapers are better for placing employer brand stories.

Pros:

- A more mature, locally targeted readership could reach older potential staff

- Less competition from other employers

- Opportunities to run local stories to build your employer brand

Cons:

- Cost can be prohibitive

- Fewer readers means fewer responses

 Tip: If you are still keen on local newspaper advertising, try an advert in other classified job sections, such as hairdressing or retail, to attract those who haven't considered care work.

 Tip: Your advert wording, particularly the title and call to action, can have a big impact on responses. See Chapter 3 for tips on wording.

Direct mail, door drops and flyers

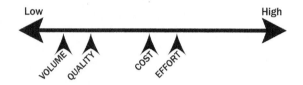

If you haven't already, I recommend plotting your existing staff's home postcodes onto a local map (Google Maps works well for this) and looking for concentrations of location pins indicating high-potential neighbourhoods for community out-reach and direct mail.

Many care providers try leafleting households in targeted neighbourhoods to generate new applicants. Results can often be disappointing because the success or failure of this method depends on getting several elements correct all at once (see below) and most recruiters fail to do this, or give up after their first attempt.

The most common method of running a leafleting campaign is as follows:

- Approach a design agency to produce a leaflet design

- Find a local distribution company and agree the drop date, quantity and areas for distribution

- Arrange for the leaflets to be printed and delivered to the distribution company

- Wait for responses

Typical distribution costs are £85 or more per thousand leaflets distributed, often excluding design and print costs, and response rates will be fractions of 1%.

Key elements in a successful door drop campaign

Audience. Targeting areas where existing staff live can be the most successful strategy. Door drop distributors can help with geodemographic postcode analysis to match likely recipients to your preferred target.

Message. This should be tailored to the problems or needs of the audience, as we saw in Chapter 3. Inviting recipients to a specific event, such as an open day, can drive more responses since it asks for a specific action to be taken.

The design of the piece should include a picture of a real care worker and an engaging headline such as 'Becoming a care worker was the best decision I ever made. Why don't you join me?' Add a clear call to action and use a real name for the recipient to call for more information or to ask questions. As we have seen already, offering a twenty-four-hour recruitment hotline is much more effective than just a 9am–5pm option.

Medium. Should you use an A5 card – perhaps double-sided? Or a letter in a 'Dear Householder' envelope? Should the distribution go out as a standalone (known as 'solus') drop or bundled with other flyers or post? There are many variables to test, but as a rule, a double-sided A5 card delivered solus yields the best response.

 Tip: Die-cutting to a non-standard shape can help you stand out.

Timing. Traditionally, there are certain times of the year when people consider a career change or returning to work. These include January and September, so careful timing could lift response rates. Repeating the same campaign at other times may see a reduced volume. With the cost of living increasing, more people are open to local, flexible work to top up household finances, so do emphasise these elements alongside the obvious altruistic factors.

Frequency. As with some other media, repeating the message can gradually improve response rates.

Distributors recommend at least three drops per campaign to maximise returns.

Pros:

- Can be highly targeted, to street level

- Will be looked at by the householder, especially if delivered on its own, so creates awareness if not a response

- Responses can happen months after the drop as recipients may keep the flyer for later action

Cons:

- Very low response rates so high volumes are needed

- Can be expensive when design, print and distribution costs are considered

- Significant effort to design, prepare and deliver

Banners

A recruitment banner is most commonly used by residential care providers who have street frontage and can be a relatively low-cost way of creating long-term awareness. It will in some cases require permission from the local council and shouldn't create a distraction to road users.

Give thought to your message. Some tips are:

- Don't add too much copy (wording), especially if the banner is going to be seen by drivers who may only have a few seconds of exposure.

- Make your message creative and engaging – too many banners say 'Hiring now'. So what? You'll get much more attention with something like 'If you worked here, your commute would be over'.

- Think about the call to action – 'Come in for a chat' is much more effective than listing an email address or phone number.

Pros:

- Once produced, a banner can be reused many times
- Very little cost
- Easy to install
- Targets locals

Cons:

- Can communicate desperation for staff
- It's passive advertising, which can quickly become 'wallpaper'

- Only effective if there is passing foot or vehicle traffic

Outdoor advertising

There will be many other opportunities to advertise in the community using a print medium, such as:

- Hospital information boards

- Doctor surgery advertising

- Display adverts in local community booklets

- Petrol pump adverts

In many cases, you will receive calls from what seems like an unending stream of eager print media sales-people claiming to offer huge reach to your target audience. As a rule, though, most of these passive print methods offer poor returns on investment. I have frequently come across providers who have paid for a range of different print adverts and either do not track the source of subsequent enquiries so have no idea if the investment worked, or have seen no discernible response. It's money down the drain.

My recommendation is to be cautious about spending on advertising via any medium that is not part of your recruitment plan. Spontaneous decisions to advertise on an ad hoc basis are almost always regretted. Having said that, some local media can be valuable awareness raisers as part of a structured campaign. Examples include sponsoring a prominent local roundabout and bus-back adverts on specific routes that pass your residential setting.

Pros:

- Can target either a locality or a certain local demographic

- Some value in raising brand awareness

Cons:

- Requires commitment with no guarantee or proof of success

- Adverts within a publication can have low visibility

Hyper-local advertising

One level down from the media that employ sales staff, there are a surprising number of what I term 'hyper-local' opportunities to advertise in any area at little or no cost.

Accessing these usually requires you to approach the media owner directly, or simply place an advert without any prior approval. While you can't expect many responses, it does all add to getting the word out into your recruitment hinterland and has the advantage of being targeted, so your message can be tailored to be of maximum interest to those who see it.

A selection of hyper-local sources that have been successful in generating applications and enquiries include:

- Parish magazines (which reach churchgoers, a high-potential target group)

- Local shops (particularly those serving a specific community where existing staff live – chip shops have been a popular option, for example)

- Hairdressers or other establishments where females gather (assuming your workforce is mainly female)

- Flyers in school bags (obviously highly targeted to parents of school-age children)

- University and college noticeboards (particularly nursing, medical and social care courses)

- Community centres, village halls, village noticeboards, communal halls in sheltered housing (targets care workers who are visiting)

- Car windscreen flyers in supermarket car parks (targeting car drivers, if this is a job requirement)

For a longer list of community opportunities, see Chapter 10.

The medium you need to use will vary, such as A6 postcards, small posters, display adverts and so on. In some cases, prior permission and payment will be required, but most hyper-local opportunities should be free or very low cost.

 Tip: My favourite format is a portrait A5 flyer with both a QR code as well as tear-off strips with contact details. Tear off the first two strips before use and this creates the impression others are interested. This is the same principle used for tip jars in cafés and coffee shops, where adding a float of coins at the beginning of the shift encourages others to follow suit.

Pros:

- Usually free or a nominal fee

- Highly targeted

- Multiple options allow aggregated returns

Cons:

- Likely to be low response rates

- Effort to seek out, post and maintain your adverts

Recruitment cards

You and your employees will come across people all the time who could make potential care staff. Why not print a stock of business cards that have a recruitment message on one side, contact details, some key benefits of care work and a space for the card holder to add their initials or name on the other side? These can be given to anyone you or your staff meet who might fit the bill. This could be an attentive waiter or waitress, a volunteer, neighbour or chance contact.

Pros:

- Simple and convenient to carry

- Can track who made the referral using the initials or name on the card, so they can be rewarded

- Empowers staff

Cons:

- Upfront print cost

- Depends on staff carrying and distributing them

Radio

Several care providers I have spoken to have tried a local radio campaign, usually persuaded to do so by a cold call from a radio station sales rep. The costs have been several thousand pounds per campaign and there has been almost universal disappointment about the results and return on investment.

As a medium for recruiting care workers, radio is poor at generating a response. There are several reasons for this. First, listeners are often busy doing something else such as driving or working so aren't immediately able to go to a website or call a telephone number. Second, in the UK we can't offer the range of stations that you would find in the US and so can't target audiences as well, meaning there is lots of wastage. Third, radio works best as part of a multimedia campaign or when your advert is repeated so often that it starts to get remembered. Either scenario will require a budget beyond most care providers.

There is evidence that radio lifts brand awareness with its listener demographic, but without some other media that provokes a response, it is an expensive and inefficient method.

Pros:

- Wide reach across a territory
- Delivers brand awareness

Cons:

- Expensive
- Requires a repeated campaign and/or multimedia commitment to be at all effective
- High wastage
- Poor conversions from call to action

Summary

- Displaying ads in local newspapers won't give you a return in most cases. Use local press to build your employer brand instead.
- Door drops are effective if you get every variable right, and they create awareness.

- There are lots more local opportunities than you might think to use printed adverts.

- Radio advertising could work, but only if it's part of a bigger multimedia campaign like mass recruitment for a large care facility opening. Otherwise, save your money.

9

The Power Of Your In-house Networks

By in-house networks, I mean the many and various social connections that are linked in at least one way to your organisation. These include my favourite recruitment source of high-quality care workers: staff referral. Since writing the first edition of this book in 2017, I have spent most of my time working on a digital solution to maximise this channel. More on that later. In research, job survival of candidates sourced from in-house networks was 24% higher than other sources.[39] I measure it at much higher than that in my experience.

In-house networks are a critical part of any care provider's recruitment strategy. In my view, if you haven't activated several sources from this channel, then it will put your entire business at risk in the coming years. Nearly thirty years ago, it was estimated that 85% of all care staff were sourced this way.[40] Since then, internet job boards have lured recruiters with their siren song of limitless flows of candidates at the click of a mouse.

I encourage readers to pay special attention to getting the most from the opportunities below.

 Tip: Watch my whiteboard video 'Using In-house Networks To Recruit' at www.savingsocialcare.com/videos

Employee referrals – recruitment gold

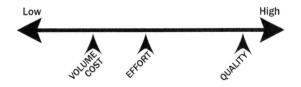

Unless you track the sources of all applicants (which I recommend) or operate an optimised employee referral scheme (ERS) or refer-a-friend programme, you may not realise that your employees could already be your best source of high-quality, long-staying new staff. Many recruiters I ask are uncertain how many new starters were recommended by staff, or rarely pay out employee referral scheme rewards. I love hearing this, as it means there is a big opportunity to improve the quality and volume of applicants.

Before we get into the 'how' of setting up and operating a successful ERS, let's start with the 'why'. Why should you be excited about getting an employee referral scheme launched, or, more commonly, relaunching a failing or neglected one?

Simply put, in almost every case, an employee referral scheme will be your most reliable source of high-quality care candidates. US research discovered that after three years, only 14% of staff who were sourced from internet job boards were still in place compared with 47% of those who joined because of an employee referral.[41]

Time and time again when I work with recruiters to map the source of their highest-performing, most reliable and long-serving staff, it is those referred by other staff members who top the list. It's time to turbo-charge these word-of-mouth referrals.

Care Friends

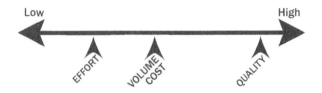

Okay. This is awkward. One of the most notable recruitment innovations since I wrote *Saving Social Care* in 2017, has been Care Friends, the rapidly growing employee referral app for care workers. Since it was my idea, it feels horribly self-serving to feature it, but if someone else had thought of it, it would definitely make it into the book, so here goes.

The app is a digitised, gamified approach to employee referral. Its main objective is simple: to encourage as many care workers as possible to become recruiters for their organisation, maximise the frequency of referring activity and enlarge the pool of referrers.

It was launched in partnership with Skills for Care in June 2020 and has demonstrated that up to 30% of all new starters can be consistently delivered via this channel. Of course, as these starters are selected by care workers, they are high converters through the recruitment funnel (typically five candidates convert to one care worker versus over eighty to one from internet job boards). Most importantly, they also have much improved tenure. Care providers report year one staff turnover of app-sourced employees at between 0% and 10% compared to a sector average of 35–50% (with rates in the 90%s for homecare not being unusual).

The app allows staff to earn points at key stages of the recruitment process, as well as for good work or an achievement. It features gamification techniques such as a leader board and digital merit badges.

As more and more care workers join the app both in the UK and Australia, we are learning much more about how to optimise and automate the platform to further increase its performance. We are still at the foothills of what is possible using gamification and behavioural science but Care Friends has already been honoured with the King's Award for Enterprise for Innovation in 2023 in recognition of its commercial success, the UK's most prestigious business award.

Employee referral scheme success factors

Only happy employees refer. Before we look at the key factors that make an employee referral scheme a success, remember that no amount of clever marketing can encourage staff to recommend job vacancies to friends if they don't feel proud to work for your organisation. If you have worked hard to get referrals and they still don't come, then it is quite likely you have a much bigger problem on your hands – staff aren't happy and they won't want their friends to suffer too.

If this sounds like your problem, then skip straight to Chapter 14. I would start by talking to staff or running a survey to understand their level of engagement and the likely cause of dissatisfaction.

For those who are confident this isn't the case in their company, let's look at the components of a successful ERS.

An attractive reward. The most common reward is £150 to £250 paid after successful probation of the referred staff member, but I recommend incentivising the effort of referring, as we'll see in a minute. It is worth asking staff to see what rewards they would value most. This could be non-monetary, such as a paid day off or first chance to book time off on public holidays, but money is universally popular and be as generous as you can. However, the amount on offer is not the main driver of referral activity.

Market to new starters. The best time to seek referrals is as early in an employee's time with you as possible. Staff who join with a friend are likely to stay longer than those who join alone.

Make it simple to refer. Don't expect staff to make all the effort in bringing their friends in.

Be respectful. Existing staff are putting their reputation at risk with both you, their employer, and their friend or contact. Do not treat these applicants in the same way as those from internet job boards. In many cases, the introduced person will want an informal chat without commitment as the first step. If you show respect to their friends, then staff will feel more loyal to you.

Should you decide not to hire a referred candidate then the referrer deserves to know the reasons why and be encouraged to think of others who might suit the role better. The more employees feel part of the process, the more successful the scheme will be.

Remove hidden handbrakes. Aside from having a poor employer reputation, which discourages referrals, perhaps staff are fearful of recommending someone and losing their own hours. Homecare providers have found that staff may be resistant to recommending friends who live nearby for fear they will have to share their nearby clients. Reassure them that their shifts, hours or clients will be protected.

Launch (or re-launch) with a fanfare. It's not enough to launch an ERS with a mention in the newsletter or a poster in the office – or even an email. Use multiple channels, such as text messages, email, Facebook, posters, payslips and team meetings, to create some buzz.

Next, make sure there is an attractive launch incentive, such as a significant prize for the first referral to be hired or double rewards for the first three months of the scheme. The goal is to get employees talking about the scheme and into the habit of referring – perhaps even competing with each other to refer.

Ensure the scheme is owned and supported by the boss. If you aren't the owner, director or senior manager, then make sure you have the right level of buy-in to launch an ERS. Where possible, get the CEO or owner to put their name to it publicly.

Keep the scheme top of mind and exciting. Ongoing successes need lots of marketing – post on Facebook, splash in the newsletter and so on. Why not try a double payment month offer ahead of holiday periods when you know you will be short-staffed?

Pay quickly. Care providers have successfully tested paying out the entire reward as soon as the referred employee starts training rather than waiting until completion of a probationary period. The benefits of encouraging more referrals by increasing participation should outweigh any risk of early drop-outs. Prompt payments help connect effort with reward and send a message that employees' efforts are appreciated and important to the organisation. Care Friends has taken this even further and facilitates micro-payments as rewards for candidate progress pre-hire.

Thank referrers with feeling. Have the CEO or owner personally call or meet each referrer to thank them for their contribution. Public praise can work well to remind others what the rewards are and recognise the organisation's gratitude. A word of warning, though – some care workers can find public praise embarrassing, or be concerned that they are seen to be earning more than colleagues, so always check first with each staff member if they are comfortable to be recognised in this way.

Tier your rewards. Offer bigger rewards to staff who successfully refer more than one new starter in a set period. For example, when an employee's second referral joins, why not pay them 1.5 times the standard reward? For a third successful referral, an extra day's holiday or other standout reward will encourage even more referrals.

Actively manage your scheme. Behind any popular ERS there is an enthusiastic administrator who keeps employees and their referred candidates up to date with the application and ensures that rewards are paid out and participants are appreciated.

Don't limit the scheme to employees. As we will discuss shortly, there are many other people connected to your organisation who will know potential staff. Could other groups participate in your ERS? For example, interviewees could recommend others and receive a reward after they join.

Employee referral scheme risks and challenges

Like every recruitment method, these schemes do come with risks and challenges. For example:

Family members. Exercise caution when hiring family members as tensions can sometimes arise if several members of one family work together in a team. You may wish to add conditions to your ERS that allow you to exclude family members if you consider this to be a risk.

More of the same. If your current workforce is not high quality or a cultural match with the organisation, then encouraging more of a similar type of person through an ERS may not be appropriate.

Pros:

- Proven, high-quality, ongoing source of candidates

- Potential to access significant new pools of candidates inaccessible by any other method

- When friends of employees join, it usually means both stay longer

- Spend on this channel goes to your own employees, not a third-party media company

Cons:

- Requires regular marketing and administration

- Family members or associated parties can be problematic

- Rejections need handling sensitively

Good leavers

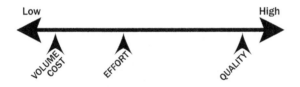

All care employers will have 'good leavers' – someone they are sorry to lose. It is a common reaction from a manager to 'write off' someone who hands in their notice and focus on replacing them. This can be a mistake. In tests in the US care market, up to 30% of good leavers returned within six months when they were regularly contacted by their manager and told they were missed. This system of staying in touch with leavers and asking if they would like to return was repeated here in the UK and similar results were found.

Why would leavers come back in such high numbers? Staff leave for many reasons. There are cases where staff have been nagged into leaving by a partner or spouse who is being inconvenienced by the work hours or continuous requests to step in to cover shifts. Perhaps they feel their partner is unappreciated. In other situations, good staff leave for a pay rise and regret their decision, but feel too embarrassed to ask to come back.

While it is most successful to activate your messages soon after staff leave, it is possible to go back through your personnel records to review all leavers in the past year and identify those you were sorry to lose, if you still have their contact details and permission to stay in touch. The most effective messages focus on the relationship staff had with those they cared for, especially if you can pass on that their clients or residents miss them.

Text messages and postcards to their home work well, as do phone calls. If you speak to the ex-employee, why not arrange to meet for a coffee to see how they are getting on? There have been examples in other sectors where meeting ex-employees in this way has resulted in a higher percentage of them agreeing to return to work.

Even if the ex-employee is unable or unwilling to return, why not ask them if they know anyone who might be interesting in joining?

 Tip: Set up a system to stay in touch with good leavers. They are an untapped source of candidates who know the organisation and those receiving care and need no settling in period.

 Tip: Ensure you ask for permission to stay in touch with employees after their employment ends.

Pros:

- Re-joiners are a known entity, need no orientation and integrate instantly

- Sends a positive message to existing staff

- Reduces your staff turnover rate

Cons:

- Some returners will leave again after a short period back, especially if there was an underlying relationship conflict that drove them away that has not since been resolved

157

Family referrals

If your organisation has been providing high-quality care to consumers for several years, then you will have built up a tremendous amount of goodwill with their families. Why not approach them to see if they know anyone who might make a suitable care worker? Research has found that approximately half of families live within 10 miles of the person being cared for and therefore have a local network.

Make sure you are not presenting this search for new staff as a matter of desperation, or implying that there is an impending shortage of staff which could affect the quality of care for the families' loved ones. Of course, approaching past consumers' families should be done sensitively, and the timing needs careful thought.

 Tip: In the US, some care providers offer incentives such as discounts off fees or several hours of free care for successful family referrals. Could this work in your situation?

Pros:

- Families know what good care is and will be careful to recommend only suitable contacts

- Goodwill means they are likely to look on your behalf

Cons:

- Where a new member of staff has a close connection to a resident or client, it may be best if they are not directly caring for that person

Referrals from applicants

Most recruiters will spend much of their time talking to applicants, either on the phone or face to face in an interview or informal chat. Why not ask those who seem suitable if they can think of similar friends who might be interested in joining? This can also be added as a question on your application form. Most candidates will be eager to please and may well recommend others as they will see this as reflecting well on their application.

Pros:

- Simple to implement
- Zero cost
- Maximises the return from your existing recruitment effort

Cons:

- Volume of referrals likely to be small
- Quality is likely to be weaker than employee referrals as the applicant does not know the values of the organisation or, in many cases, the requirements of the role

Those who reject your job offer

Considering the competition for applicants on internet job boards and how easy it is for applicants to apply for multiple jobs, you will be processing a good number of applicants who will be courted by many other employers at the same time. This will lead to interview no-shows, apparent disinterest and those who reject you or simply do not respond after you've offered them the role.

If you make a job offer and it is rejected, it is natural to write off that candidate. However, quality applicants will not be short of offers and may choose a competitor for reasons they come to regret. Certainly, if they're courteous enough to call and decline your offer, be gracious in defeat and keep the door open. Diarise to call or text them after two weeks and then again at two months and six months to see how they are getting on. Perhaps that salary offer never materialised or they are feeling unappreciated. At worst you will be seen as a caring employer, and you may well find they would like to reconsider their decision. Even if they are not open to joining after six months, add them to your candidate database for the future.

Pros:

- Applicant quality will be high as you have been prepared to make an offer

- Can mean you get a second bite of the cherry, with very low additional recruitment and screening effort

- Adds to your word-of-mouth reputation as a good employer

Cons:

- Difficult to overcome the annoyance of being rejected first time around

- May indicate the candidate is a timewaster or lacks commitment

Stakeholder networks

All care businesses have a network of stakeholders – those in the community who support or have dealings with them. We have discussed some of the more obvious groups, such as staff and families, but you could be surprised by the other local connections who, if asked, might put the word out to find care staff for you.

These could include:

- Trustees or board members

- Other care providers you work with

- Accountants

- Taxi firms

- Local suppliers

- Consultants

- Visiting healthcare professionals

- Training organisations

 Tip: Review your visitors' book or supplier list to build a database of people and organisations that regularly interact with your company. Who 'owes you'?

Pros:

- Taps into social networks that you may not normally reach

- Stakeholders will often go out of their way to help

- They're likely to screen on your behalf and only suggest those they consider to be suitable candidates

Cons:

- Likely to be a trickle of candidates, maybe even none in a year

- Requires you to ask a favour of people you may not know personally

Summary

- Offer an employee referral scheme and run it well.

- Cut your staff turnover by up to 30% by asking good leavers to come back.

- Enlist clients' families to look out for candidates for you.

- Ask all interviewees, 'Do you know anyone else suitable?'

- Don't brood if your job offer is rejected. Stay in touch. You never know.

10
Community Networking

Community networking is something of a for-gotten skill. With the increasing pressure on recruiters and care managers, it can be hard to find the time to leave the office and engage with local people and potential partner organisations around you. But this channel, like those networks that are directly connected to your organisation, is a great source of high-quality potential staff. It reaches out to passive job seekers – those who could make excellent care staff if only it was suggested to them.

There are many sources of community networking in your local area. In this section, I will pick some of my favourites.

Unpaid carers

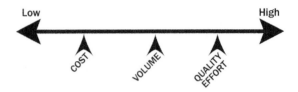

Unpaid or family carers represent a largely untapped and high-quality source of future paid care staff. In the UK, there were about seven million family carers, or one in ten of the population,[42] pre-Covid-19. This number will have increased significantly due to the long-term effects of the virus and mental and physical health deterioration across the population, particularly amongst those already frail and vulnerable.

We know from research in the US that over 40% of those whose family care duties have ended would consider carrying on their care work in a paid capacity.[43] So, there is the potential to bring into the paid workforce large numbers of people with valuable hands-on skills and experience who want to continue to gain the intrinsic rewards they discovered from caring for a loved one.

Our challenge is to identify and engage with these carers, who are often isolated at home. Some do attend support networks where they can meet other carers. Care providers in the US market have successfully engaged with these groups by offering them free spaces on training days, such as for moving and handling, then word-of-mouth referrals can naturally happen. You may find there is a gatekeeper or organiser of your local carer group, and your ability to engage this group may depend on how supportive this individual is of your overtures.

Another source are hospices; I cover those in Chapter 11.

Pros:

- Family care experience is very highly correlated with success in a paid care role

- Huge numbers of those in your local community, young and old, have cared for a loved one and so have experienced the intrinsic rewards of the role

Cons:

- Hard to reach this group as they can be isolated or not mention their unpaid care role when applying for a role

- Unpaid carers can lack self-confidence and consider themselves unemployable

Faith-based sources

There is a clear connection between those who worship and caring for others. Polls in the US homecare sector found 84% of care workers actively worshipped.[44] Many of our longest established care providers are faith-based, and faiths of all denominations are active in their local communities supporting the sick and vulnerable. The best ways to approach faith-based recruitment include using existing staff connections, offering to talk at gatherings, sponsoring, volunteering, fund-raising, taking a stand at an event, advertising in the newsletter or on a notice-board. There are more faith-based organisations in your local community than simply places of worship. An example in the UK is the Salvation Army.

Although it's not always easy to engage religious organisations, faith-based recruiting should be an element of any community outreach strategy.

Pros:

- Compassion and giving are fundamental values of most of those who worship

- Places of worship are easy to find and are often hubs of community activity

Cons:

- Recruiting heavily from a single religion can cause rostering challenges on their day of worship

- Sometimes tricky to get accepted as faith settings can be cautious of commercial approaches

- Some devout worshippers may feel compelled to spread the word to those they care for

Cause-related sources

Not-for-profit causes are another local source that can bring you into contact with people who put others before themselves. Examples include:

- Chronic diseases support groups: Parkinson's, Alzheimer's, etc

- Cancer charities, especially Breast Cancer UK and Macmillan Nurses

- Those groups with which your staff have a personal connection or allegiance

- Red Cross

- Age UK

- Hospital friends

- British Legion

- Rotary Club

In most cases, giving either time, money or some other tangible support to the cause is the best way to build relationships.

Pros:

- These are target groups with an affinity for caring

- Partnership can lead to further opportunities

Cons:

- Approaches from commercial organisations can be viewed with scepticism by some charities

- Success often dependent on the support of local charity management

Interest groups with mature and/or female members

If you have identified common interests, hobbies or demographic profiles that are over-represented in your higher-performing staff, then seek out places in the community where similar people gather. Research indicates that older people or females are two such groups, so if I were looking in the community to find those demographics, the following would be some of my targets:

- Women's Institute

- Local historical societies

- Knitting clubs

- Book clubs

- The local women's football team (consider sponsoring)

- Craft fairs (popular with nurses, for reasons beyond me)

Pros:

- Can be opportunities to speak about care work, or have a presence or sponsorship

Cons:

- Often difficult to get accepted without a previous connection or introduction

Animal lovers

Several care employers have found a high proportion of animal lovers in their staff. When I ask at care conferences who owns a dog, it is usually half the audience, whereas dog ownership nationally is half that, at 24% of households.[45] Those who care for horses also seem over-represented.

My guess is those who care for animals (and dogs need more attention than cats, and those who look after horses have to get up at 5am every day, regardless of the weather) may have a higher likelihood of also caring for people. This would suggest it could be worth advertising in or networking with the following:

- Veterinary surgeries

- Animal charities

- Pet events

- Dog training courses

- Striking up conversations with dog walkers

- Equestrian events

Pros:

- This is a large group – an animal lover can be found in almost every park or recreation ground

Cons:

- The link between a love of animals and suitability for caring is not clear cut, and some providers report that pet owners prioritise their animals over humans

- Animal owners may not want to leave their pets for an extended time, which will restrict their work availability

Community locations

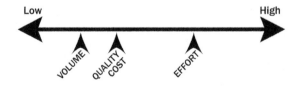

High-visibility sites exist in all towns and cities, and are opportunities for networking, displaying a poster or running an outreach event or stand. Many in the list below would particularly attract an older and/or female visitor, if these were targets you had identified as your priority:

- Post Offices

- Coffee shops

- Cafés and restaurants (target good waiting staff)

- Hairdressers

- Community or village halls / groups

- Libraries

- Leisure centres

- School bag newsletters

- Car park windscreen leaflet drops (check permissions, and only do this when rain is not forecast)

- Sponsored supermarket till bag packing with a charity partner (or your own organisation directly if not-for-profit)

- Fast food outlets, including fish and chip shops

- Women's refuges

- Social services

- Garden centres

- Doctors surgeries

- Clinics

- Physiotherapists

- Pharmacies

- Opticians

- Social clubs

- Newsagents

- Bingo halls

- Bowls clubs

- Bridge clubs

- Mobility shops (targets existing carers)

- Local websites or Facebook community pages

- Allotment noticeboards

- Public transport hubs

- Charity shops

Pros:

- With such a wide range of options there will always be some venues that can be successfully targeted

- Often not considered by competitors

Cons:

- Requires effort and time to approach each one

- Most will probably not deliver any applicants and so there is a lot of trial and error

Community events

In addition to permanent community locations, you can target events. Most of these will happen in the summer months, so plan ahead. Take a stand, run a competition, sponsor, or simply go along to network.

Why not try the following?

- Car boot sales

- Jumble sales

- Markets

- Charity events

- Summer fayres

- Blood donation centres (people might sign anything, like a contract of employment, as they recover from giving blood!)

- Dog and horse shows

Pros:

- Often low cost to have a stand

- The reach to local people can be high

- Can create awareness even if people don't stop to speak to you

- Face-to-face contact is a powerful way of selling care work and building relationships

Cons:

- Requires willing employees to staff the stand

- Investment needed to buy a stand and materials to engage visitors, if not already purchased

- Success dependent on factors outside your control, such as the weather and volume of visitors

Rural residents

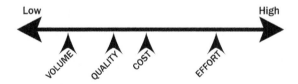

In rural areas, recruiters can often be at a loss as to how to find new staff, but even in these sparsely populated areas, opportunities exist. It is true that reaching those living rurally requires you to invest time, but once they're recruited, rural care staff can be long-stayers with your organisation.

The following are examples of places where care providers can either advertise or network to find new recruits:

- Hubs where the community might gather, such as village halls, pubs, the Post Office, convenience shops or churches

- A poster on a village or school notice board, at bus stops, in village halls or near road junctions (if safe and permission is obtained)

- Online community forums such as Facebook pages

- Events such as exercise classes, concerts, fayres or walking groups

- Local newsletters and village magazines

- Advertising on supermarket petrol pumps is a good way of reaching drivers who travel in from the countryside to refuel or shop

Pros:

- Rural dwellers will most likely run a car given their isolation, so will have transport

- Can be more loyal as they are less targeted by other employers

- For homecare providers, this group may be more resilient when having to drive on dark country roads to visit consumers than urban dwellers

Cons:

- An effort to find them

Newcomers to the area

Targeting new entrants to the community who might need local work is a niche recruitment strategy, but one that can yield good results. Most adults in the UK only move eight times in their lifetime,[46] so the likely opportunity for finding many new staff this way is relatively small.

Methods of reaching this group include:

- Leaflet drops in new-build affordable housing

- Leaflet drops in target communities where there is a 'Sold' estate agent sign

- Approaching housing associations and estate agents/rental agents

- The Royal Mail home-movers data (available for a fee in the UK – the minimum dataset is 5,000, so may be limited to large urban areas)

Pros:

- Movers new to the area will likely need local work

Cons:

- Hard to spot newcomers at the time they arrive

- Can be scattered across your territory randomly

- A tiny niche of potential applicants

Competitors' staff

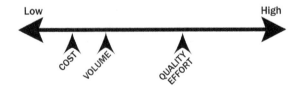

Although I do not encourage targeted 'poaching' of other local care staff since we all must be focused on growing the workforce for the benefit of all rather than swapping employees between providers, we will have applicants who currently work for a local care provider. However, many employers I speak to are perplexed because, despite them having a good reputation and paying more than others in the local market, they find it hard to attract local care staff.

There are several reasons for this. Good care staff will often be loath to abandon those they care for, regardless of their dissatisfaction with their current employer. The worker–client bond is usually much stronger than that between the worker and their supervisor or employer. There is also an element of inertia, or a fear that things will be worse if they move and lose coveted shifts or routes that suit their lifestyle.

Moves can be triggered by a manager changing jobs and enticing staff to follow, or when there is an unsettling change at the workplace. Other methods of attracting in-post staff to join could include:

- Offer free giveaways to any local care worker, such as 'posh' coffee, de-icer or car scrapers in the winter

- Advertise on sheltered housing notice boards (targets visiting care workers)

- Wait outside large sheltered housing facilities and approach care staff

- Facebook targeted advertising

- Offer welcome (sign-on) bonuses to overcome the loss of income during training

- In homecare, win new clients with a personal budget to bring their care worker team across to your employment

- CV search

Pros:

- Targets experienced applicants

Cons:

- Deliberate targeting of a competitor's staff can create ill will and the potential for tit-for-tat reprisals against your organisation

- Some paid care staff can bring bad habits and poor attitudes

Volunteers

Those who give their time for free represent great potential recruits, especially if the cause they are supporting is connected to caring in some way. The three most likely types of recruits amongst volunteers are those raising money for a cause in the street (excluding paid street fundraisers), those working in charity shops and those active on community projects.

 Tip: Prepare a small business card saying, 'You could be our next care worker' and give them to staff to hand out when they meet someone like this. See 'Recruitment cards' in Chapter 8.

Pros:

- Volunteers often have the right attitude for care work

Cons:

- Approaching volunteers in the street or in a charity shop about care work requires some confidence

Open days

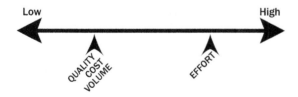

Open days are much easier for on-site residential care settings than for community-based providers as they have a ready-made venue. An open day can be an effective way of engaging with the local community and encouraging interest from potential staff who may pass your care setting every day but otherwise have no reason or invitation to make contact.

The success of open days is entirely dependent on you generating interest ahead of the event, which is often down to a motivated and enthusiastic organiser and targeted multi-channel marketing. There is a cost to preparing materials, banners, flyers, other advertising and refreshments, but some marketing can be undertaken on social media, which costs nothing. Open days are most suitable for mass recruitment tied to the opening or launch of a new service, where there could be high levels of local awareness and support from the media. Why not host a dog competition to bring in animal lovers?

Pros:

- Low cost if you can use your premises

- Improves local awareness even if attendance is disappointing

- Can be popular with staff and residents

Cons:

- Less relevant for community-based services such as homecare

- Difficult to predict demand

- Requires marketing and organisation effort

Walk-ins

Walk-ins are speculative applicants. As a recruit-ment source, they have similarities with open days, although there is little cost or effort involved in gen-erating walk-ins. The number of walk-ins you will have is highly dependent on your office or setting location. If you are on a major transport route with easy parking or in an urban centre then walk-ins can be frequent. However, many homecare businesses have relocated to lower-cost office accommodation in business parks or the upper floors of commercial buildings and so have less opportunity to encounter this type of applicant.

It is important to think about how to encourage walk-ins, for example where you place signage, and what the process is if someone presents themselves at the door. Staff should ensure that their welcome is friendly, and they take contact details if there is no one available to meet the applicant at that time. A per-centage of walk-ins will be those who are referred by members of staff and so this can be a quality source.

 Tip: Just using a sign saying 'Jobs' and an arrow can be effective.

Pros:

- Can include those referred by others, so well worth gearing up to handle walk-ins if feasible

- Little cost and effort

Cons:

- No control over volume and timing

- Highly dependent on your location, visibility and ease of access

Shopping centre or supermarket outreach

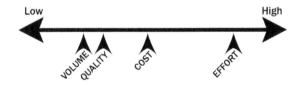

If I were to summarise the feedback from all care providers who have shared the results of their shopping centre or supermarket outreach efforts, then I would have to say it is disappointing, although there are some enthusiasts.

Taking a stand or pop-up concession in a shopping centre or supermarket will probably incur a fee payable to the centre management or a third-party company. There will also be regulations and restrictions, such as how far you can stand from your station, and some supermarkets might consider your aim of recruiting care workers a potential threat.

Other costs will include display materials and paying staff to be present at the stand, as well as providing promotional items or activities to create some interest. Some staff will be ideal for this type of outreach work, but others may be too shy or embarrassed and so it is not wise to press-gang people into being involved.

Results seem to be best when stands are manned by genuine care staff rather than the office or admin team. Once your stand is on-site, there certainly is an art to engaging members of the public in conversation. Consider the location, particularly in supermarkets, as shoppers may not wish to stop and talk if they have a trolley full of frozen goods.

You will need to ensure a good flow of people; this suggests weekends would be the best time, which can be a challenge to staff. Shopping centres will have a certain target audience, based on the location, type of retail units and the time of day and day of the week.

It is critical to ensure that all leads are followed up quickly after the event. It is surprising how often this is forgotten or delayed.

Pros:

- Can create awareness even if people don't stop to speak to you

- Face-to-face contact is a powerful way of selling care work and building relationships

- Ask everyone you speak to for a referral too

Cons:

- Expensive

- Requires planning and effort

- Requires willing staff to man the stand

Summary

- Build relationships with your local family carer group as they are some of the best future staff.

- Anyone who actively worships will likely be compassionate and giving.

- Support a related cause to help build your employer brand and put you in contact with likeminded people.

- People who care for animals are likely to care for people too.

- Get out of the office and attend community events. Let people know you exist.

11
Widening Your Search

Closely related to community outreach is seeking out organisations locally that could connect you with suitable future staff. There are a range of organisations, some quite unexpected, which can help with your search for new employees.

Other great contributors to the social care workforce are migrants. Some employers, particularly in urban centres, can be dependent on migrants and ethnic groups, so it is important to understand how to make the most of this opportunity, especially as migration to the UK has fundamentally changed in recent years.

Let's start with partner organisations and consider the more prominent ones.

Job centres and long-term unemployed work programmes

I want to be positive about recruiting the unemployed and those on benefits into care work. It should be a success story given the low qualification requirements, flexible local work and comprehensive training on offer by care employers, but, with a few heart-warming exceptions, it is usually a waste of a recruiter's time. In a poll of 3,000 care workers undertaken by the Department of Health and Social Care in 2018, just 1% gave their previous occupation as unemployed.[47] The main complaint from employers is that some of those supposedly looking for work have little intention of getting a job and are merely demonstrating job-seeking effort. There is also an all-time low unemployment level, limiting this channel further.

Where there have been successes, these seem to be down to supportive job centre staff who pre-screen candidates to be suitable and motivated for a care role themselves or by using *I Care... Ambassadors* (see Appendix 2).

Government long-term unemployed work pro-grammes can also have diligent and helpful (and perhaps financially incentivised) account managers who see a natural fit in some clients they are trying to place. Without that, the hit rate from these sources is very low – so much so that many employers have decided they simply cannot afford the opportunity cost of time spent on this source.

 Tip: Work with job centre staff to spot high-potential job seekers that fit your exact target. This could save missing those rare 'diamonds'.

Pros:

- Can work where the local job centre staff pre-screen for you

- Occasionally a quality candidate can be found

- No financial outlay and, in many cases, a financial incentive to hire

Cons:

- Usually a very low hit rate of suitable candidates

- A significant percentage of those booked for interview will not show, or if they do will be unprepared, lack motivation or be unpresentable

- Applicants may be restricted to working a limited number of hours to protect state benefits

- Many candidates will not have access to a reliable car, which can restrict the type of care work they can undertake or be otherwise not 'job ready' for a demanding care role

Job fairs

Job fairs can be organised by a range of community partners, most commonly the local authority, but the principle is that local employers are invited to participate in a shared event where those looking for a job or considering a change of career, or perhaps school-leavers, are encouraged to attend. Results from job fairs can be positive, especially if your organisation has the resources, time and staff to participate and it is publicised well. However, overall outcomes tend to be disappointing, mainly down to low attendance or poor candidate suitability and the likelihood that attendees will register with multiple employers and so be in demand.

Tip: Be completely clear about what jobs you have available so attendees are left in no doubt what you can offer. Try to differentiate yourself from other employers. Why would I choose you?

 Tip: Choose your most outgoing staff to attend. The best representatives are always those doing the job now.

 Tip: Produce eye-catching materials, and ensure your staff take details of all visitors to add to your candidate pool – even if they are not suitable, perhaps they will know someone who is.

 Tip: One word – cupcakes.

Pros:

- Event marketing is the responsibility of the organiser

- May be able to offer screening interviews at the event and so speed up the application process

- Can help your employer brand awareness even if the number of face-to-face interactions is low

- Opportunity to network with other employers

Cons:

- Attendance can be low

- Quality and motivation of job seekers can be disappointing

- Requires staffing and some costs for a stand, promotional materials and incentives

Universities

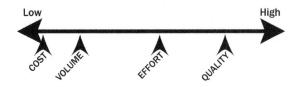

Many care employers are divided on whether students make good workers or not. As with most things, the answer is not a simple yes or no. The best successes have been with students on a related or relevant course, and the ones that are repeatedly mentioned include nursing, medicine, physiotherapy and other allied healthcare professions, social work and psychology.

Research by Leading Homecare in the US[48] found that student nurses topped the list of quality sources of homecare staff. My own research indicates a lot of positive feedback from care employers who have student nurses on their books in the UK too. This group is committed to a caring career and welcomes relevant work experience. Could time spent with your organisation be included as part of their course assessment?

 Tip: Often, an informal approach works better than the university's official channels. Methods to try include:

- Approaching the Student Welfare Officer
- Advertising on halls of residence noticeboards
- Offering to talk about social care settings
- Word-of-mouth referral from existing student nurses you have on your staff

The following pros and cons assume you have targeted students studying a healthcare or related discipline.

Pros:

- Committed and enthusiastic
- Willing to work unsociable hours around their lectures
- Will know others like them so can be great referrers
- Often very popular with clients, residents and older staff members

Cons:

- Often only available during term time and for the duration of their studies

- University admin or careers offices may have multiple approaches or be too busy to help

- Only a viable option if you have a university, especially one that trains nurses, in your locality

Vocational courses and sector training providers

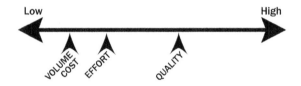

In other countries, such as the US and Australia, providers and colleges training young people in vocational social care are seen as the main route into care. This isn't the case in the UK, where either training is already aligned to an employer or vocational students can see social care as a last resort option after failing to get on a beauty, hairdressing or similar course. Their motivation to pursue a career in social care after completing their studies can be less than you might think.

Pros:

- Trained applicants

- Many will be seeking a career in the sector

Cons:

- Motivation is not always what you expect

- Need a college or training provider local to you

Hospices

Most areas of the UK are served by a hospice. These organisations usually have a large and committed supporters' group, many of whom have cared for a loved one who has since died. By sponsoring or partnering with the hospice, you can meet and talk to this supporters' group about the benefits of becoming a care worker.

Pros:

- Highly targeted group of those who have care experience

- Further opportunities to partner with hospices, such as shared training and outreach activity

Cons:

- Some of those you approach may have recently suffered a bereavement

- The hospice may be cautious of commercial approaches or see a care provider as a potential poacher of staff

Military bases

Low   High

VOLUME COST   EFFORT   QUALITY

Like universities with nursing courses, military bases are not in everyone's backyard, but if you have one then the families of military personnel can be a source of reliable staff. The obvious downside is that Forces staff regularly move and so this creates an in-built churn from this source. However, there are several positives.

The base support team is often receptive to finding external employment for military families. There is also a strong sense of community leading to word-of-mouth referral opportunities.

Military families tend to have a support structure, which can help overcome childcare challenges, and most have a stable and disciplined personal life compared to many civilians.

Pros:

- Bases will have an interest in finding employment for families

- Military way of life is disciplined and reliable

- Support from the community to cover childcare

Cons:

- Personnel regularly move to take up new roles

Public speaking

This is in the partners section because you need an organisation to invite you to speak with a membership or audience that wants to hear about care work. You might be surprised at the number of local opportunities to talk about your work. You will be considered an expert in social care when compared to the general public, even if you don't feel like one.

Here are a few places to try, but there will be many more:

- Women's Institute

- Church groups

- Schools and colleges

- Rotary clubs

- Dementia Friends meetings

- University of the Third Age

- Business Breakfast Networking clubs

Not all of us jump at the chance to stand up in front of an audience, but if you are willing to try it is a great way to get the word out to many people at once.

Pros:

- You never know who you can reach – audience members may tell their family and friends about care work

- Usually free

- Great awareness raising even if you get no direct leads

Cons:

- Not everyone is comfortable with public speaking

- Time out of the office

- Needs rehearsing and preparation

Permanent recruitment agencies

As professional recruiters, agencies often have access to a large candidate database and network and so can supply staff that you may not have otherwise reached. However, they do suffer from a poor reputation with care providers. This is somewhat unfair in many cases, but it is easy to set up shop in the recruitment market, so social care employers report hard sell techniques, with the recruiter being more interested in a sale than in quality, and being charged high fees for average or poor candidates.

If you can find a quality recruitment company, then they can add enormous value and save a lot of time and effort. The permanent placement market in social care is mainly for supervisory or management roles, with the bulk of frontline staff being temporary workers supplied to residential settings, which we will consider next.

Pros:

- Good agencies can access a candidate market you may not otherwise reach

- Candidates should be screened and therefore of better quality

Cons:

- Unscrupulous players have created a poor reputation

- Fees can be high

- Motivation of many agencies is to place candidates rather than ensure the best fit with your organisation and the role

Temp to perm

Temporary staffing agencies do not have a good reputation with residential care providers (they are rarely used in the homecare sector). During and post-Covid-19 there were widespread examples of profiteering and, in my view, many of these agencies have become greedy and contribute to the structural problems in our sector. Not all agencies are bad actors, but we desperately need price controls or fee caps to rein in their worst excesses.

If you are a residential care provider with agency staff on site for twelve weeks, they should be able to join your company if you both agree. Keep this in mind as a source. Not all agency staff want to remain peripatetic.

Pros:

- Try before you buy

- Ends agency costs for that worker

Cons:

- Many agency staff choose temporary work for the flexibility or higher pay, so conversion rates can be low

More partner organisations

There are many other potential partner groups in the community. Here is a selection, but it is certainly not an exhaustive list:

- Large employers of shift workers such as factories, where the flexible hours of care work may appeal to their partners

- Domestic abuse refuges, which may want to find flexible work for the women in their care

- Outplacement services and businesses making staff redundant, such as retail outlets closing down

- Language schools that will have a flow of recently arrived migrants

Health and Social Care Apprenticeship training providers can help you bring young people into the company. However, many smaller providers have not engaged in the scheme fully, and many apprentices are already employed by an organisation rather than new to care. Skills for Care is working to improve the scheme and more information can be found on its website.[49]

Migrants, ethnic communities and overseas recruitment

Migrants make up a significant and valuable proportion of frontline care workers in any developed society. They are a diverse and complex population, so in order to simplify the options open to a recruiter, I have split them into two broad groups: those already domiciled in the country and those who can be recruited directly from overseas.

Migrants already living here

In certain areas, typically urban areas and major cities, there will be communities of a common ethnicity, which could be valuable recruiting grounds. Ethnic groups are diverse, and the best approach to recruiting from their members will be highly localised to your setting. In the UK, 14% of the over-eighteen population is non-white, weighted to the major cities. Black and ethnic care workers are proportionately more at 23%,[50] with a strong concentration in London (over 50% of care staff).

Each major ethnic group will have its own characteristics, which can help inform your recruitment approach. For example, the Black/Caribbean population in the UK is now ageing, having its roots in post-war migration in the 1950s and 1960s, whereas the Black/African population is a more youthful and fast growing community (three-fifths have come to the UK since 1990).

Pakistani/Bangladeshi communities are often younger than the overall UK population, reflecting high fertility rates. There are also sizeable communities of Eastern Europeans, most notably from Poland, who tend to be younger. Poles still form the largest single foreign-born group in the UK, estimated in 2021 at over 696,000, despite significant reductions due to EU immigration restrictions.[51]

The best approach to engage any ethnic group is to ask existing staff who come from that group what methods they would recommend. Some approaches to consider include:

- Identify community groups and charities, eg social groups, job and skills clubs, women's groups, that work with or have members from the target group and could help you to develop opportunities for making them aware of care work.

- Write to community and religious leaders to ask them if you can speak about care work to community members seeking work. Local area development and residents' groups in target geographic areas may also be helpful.

- Work with facilities that have a high number of visitors from your target audience – a cultural or education centre, or youth or older persons' centre.

- Involve umbrella voluntary organisations as they may be able to flag to relevant volunteers either directly or through newsletters – for example, they could involve mentors working with recent immigrants or young people.

- Local businesses such as ethnic food stores, restaurants, hair salons and venues may be able to assist in spreading the message via notice boards or leaflets.

- Take a stand at a cultural event.

If you can put up posters or deliver leaflets, consider having these translated into the ethnic group's local language, while making it clear that written and spoken English will be required to an acceptable standard.

 Tip: Ensure your recruitment process is not discriminatory. James Sage, Employment Partner in RWK Goodman LLP and Head of Health and Social Care, has provided some guidance in Appendix 3.

Pros:

- Very strong for word-of-mouth referrals

- Often a cultural bias toward caring for others

Cons:

- Some communities can be wary of outside approaches

- Cultural norms may restrict what personal care tasks female staff feel comfortable doing

Importing migrant workers

Many care employers are considering, or already actively recruit, workers directly from overseas. For employers in wealthy or rural areas, it can seem like the only viable way of building a workforce. Live-in care providers relied almost entirely on this method of recruitment before Brexit. Now, many have shifted their recruitment domestically, targeting either UK-born staff or those with the right to remain in the UK or a suitable visa class.

At the time of writing, the UK social care sector is coming to terms with recent changes to visa regulations. This has opened up the opportunity to apply for sponsor licences for foreign nationals meeting the immigration criteria set by the Home Office.

This is certainly a frustrating, high-cost and bureaucratic process, with significant administrative and pastoral care burdens for the employer, such as arranging accommodation, transport, settling in, socialisation and familiarisation with language, food and customs.

By the time you read this, the situation may have changed, so I recommend checking the Skills for Care website (www.skillsforcare.org.uk), as a useful source of the latest guidance.

Putting aside immigration requirements, there is, in theory at least, an almost unlimited supply of foreign workers willing and motivated to travel abroad to work. Many countries have either a strong work ethic or a culture of familial care for elders, which has built migrants' reputations amongst employers as hard-working, reliable and compassionate frontline employees.

For me, despite the significant contribution of migrant workers to the social care sector, I have concerns over the ethics of draining feeder countries of their healthcare staff, especially as most G20 countries are following the same strategy.

Pros:

- A reputation for hard work and reliability
- Often a cultural bias toward caring for others
- An unlimited supply of potential workers

Cons:

- Recruitment and on-boarding costs can be high
- Language and cultural differences with consumers and other staff can create problems
- Immigration restrictions apply and are subject to political change
- Migrants are highly mobile so can leave at short notice

Your optimum sourcing strategy

We have reviewed a lot of potential places to find new staff, so how do we make sense of all these choices and decide which to target?

In 2022, Skills for Care asked 650 managers to name one recruitment activity that has worked well for them in the previous twelve months. Here is what they said, represented as a word cloud:

What we can see here is a major shift toward favouring passive job seeker sources, notably employee referral schemes (both 'Refer a friend' and Care Friends fit this category) but also social media and word of mouth.

The following matrix tells a similar story and displays most of the major sources we have covered on two axes: quality and volume, split into active and passive job seekers.

This matrix tells us two important things. First, passive job seeker sources, such as community outreach and employee referral, consistently deliver a better quality of candidate, albeit at much lower volumes. Second, pre-screening is essential when handling applicants from active job seeker sources.

My recommendation is to introduce screening to your high-volume, poorer quality sources, which will free up time to work on nurturing as many passive job seekers as possible from the community around you.

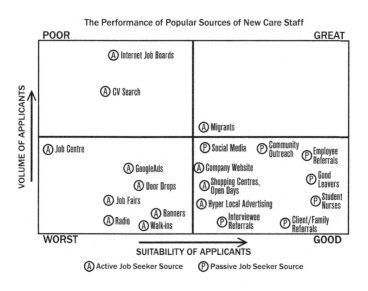

Performance of popular sources of new care workers

My favourite sources are:

- A well-promoted and efficiently run employee referral scheme

- Student nurses, if you are lucky enough to have them locally

- Asking those who have left to return

- Community outreach for both employer branding and direct application

If you know your candidate experience is poor, then work to remove log-jams, which will be making any outreach work inefficient. Also ensure you are capturing enough data to measure the success of new sources you try.

Above all, always measure the results of your sourcing activity.

A word about attribution

One of the problems with attempting to measure recruitment channel performance is that the prospective applicant can be exposed to several 'nudges' to apply prior to selecting the final method they make contact by. For example, a recommendation from a friend might result in a website application. Repeated exposure to Facebook posts might trigger a walk-in. Always try to ask how many ways the candidate heard of your company.

Summary

- Time spent on job centre recruitment without intensive pre-screening of candidates could be better used elsewhere.

- Got a university training nurses in your area? Get there before your competitors do.

- Make friends with your hospice – its supporters' group is one of the most qualified sources of new staff.

- Migrants are crucial, but expect workers you import to need lots of ongoing support.

- The recruitment market has shifted to targeting passive applicants. Ensure your recruitment strategy reflects this.

PART THREE
RETAINING

Our compliance and inspection regime has pre-occupied care managers with striving to be outstanding providers. But what about being outstanding employers?

12
Staff Turnover

Our sector suffers from chronically high staff turnover, with unnecessary numbers of resignations or dismissals. Before we start dissecting what is going on, let's be clear about how we define 'staff turnover'.

Turnover is expressed as a percentage of your total workforce that leaves in a specific period, most commonly twelve months. The way to calculate it is to add the number of staff at the beginning of the year to the number at the end and divide by two. This gives the average number of staff during that year. Then divide the total number of leavers in the same period by this average, as shown in the formula below. That is your staff turnover, expressed as a percentage.

> ### Total leavers in twelve months
> ---
> ### (Staff on day 1 + staff on day 365)/2

You can split staff turnover into two main types: voluntary and involuntary. Let's learn more about what each means.

Voluntary turnover

This is generally a bad thing, but it is not always within your control. Uncontrollable voluntary turnover includes staff retiring, moving out of the area by choice and disgruntled staff resigning. Even those being promoted out of your frontline workforce are 'leavers' from the pool of workers you are tracking, albeit not from the organisation.

Losing good employees we don't want to lose, also known as 'regrettable' turnover or 'good leavers', will be our focus. We will look at how to reduce regrettable turnover in detail, but to complicate matters further, some of it is not as bad as it seems. What if you lose a member of staff because they are qualifying as a nurse after the support and coaching they've received over several years with your organisation? Is that 'regrettable'? It certainly does your reputation no harm, and may attract more applicants than you need to replace the one you've just lost.

I said voluntary turnover is *generally* a bad thing. There are cases when it is the opposite. For example, it includes leavers you are about to dismiss who resign before they are fired. This saves you effort, stress, admin and probably money. Also, reaching zero turnover may mean you are stuck with staff set in their ways and resistant to change.

Involuntary turnover

Mostly, involuntary turnover is employment termination against the employee's wishes. Much of this can be attributed to hiring mistakes, but it could also be due to weak or non-existent pre-employment screening, or poor sourcing.

Across all UK employment sectors, the average annual staff turnover is now between 15–17%,[52] so nearly one in five staff members leave their jobs every year. Approximately 11% is voluntary turnover and 7% involuntary. The staff turnover rate of directly employed care workers working in the adult social care sector in England was estimated at 36.1% as of 2021/22. Skills for Care made this estimate using the Adult Social Care Workforce Data Set (ASC-WDS), which covers around half of the entire adult social care sector.

In US studies, most nursing homes and home health agencies were found to be dramatically underestimating the extent of their turnover problem[53] and, from my experience, this is likely being repeated in the UK.

Currently, US homecare annual turnover is reported at over 65.2%,[54] for example. My estimate, based on my work with care employers of all types, is that the UK figure of 36.1% is an optimistic one. This could be partly due to a dataset that includes local authority retention figures, which are usually much better than the independent sector, and a desire by some providers not to present a picture of high turnover when reporting figures. But equally, during the data collection period there has been a rapid increase in vacant posts (up 52% in one year).[55] This is not a stable situation.

Having said that, I have met care providers who have achieved an annual staff turnover of zero, although I could count them on the fingers of one hand. Many lose over half their staff every year, and some record annual turnover rates of over 100%. This doesn't mean they lose everyone each year; it is usually that they experience a high staff loss in the first few weeks and months of employment and then it settles down, with a percentage of loyal, committed staff managing to stay at least a year or more. In fact, *when* turnover happens in your organisation is what I want to explore next.

When does turnover happen?

I recommend that you measure staff turnover across three distinct phases of the employee lifecycle. This is important because, as we will explore in the coming chapters, different interventions are required at different stages. Someone walking out on day two of training will likely be quite a different situation to a loyal employee shocking you by handing their notice in after four years. The three phases I use are:

1. **From job offer acceptance to Day 1.** This period does not appear in the official statistics on staff turnover and yet employers are likely leaking 20–40% of those who accept their job offers but never arrive for induction training. While time taken to undertake regulatory screening requirements such as police checks and taking steps to ensure they only employ 'fit and proper' staff increase the risk of drop-outs, there is much an employer can do to minimise this loss. This will be explored in the next chapter.

2. **The first ninety days of employment.** If I had to predict where the main turnover issues lie with any care provider – and by extension, the sector as a whole – it is in this period. If all employers took steps to reduce their unnecessary first three-month staff loss by even 10%, annual turnover figures would tumble. This is because staff turnover during this period is extraordinarily high – up to half of all new starters can be lost

within these early weeks. This is most keenly felt in community-based roles such as homecare, but the main culprit across all employers is a flawed sourcing strategy, as we will see. Specifically, repeatedly hiring those who have weak job attachment in the first place. If that is the case, it is simply a matter of time before job dissatisfaction overcomes job motivation.

3. **From day ninety-one onward.** Once the high-risk settling-in period has passed, a whole range of factors affecting turnover come into play, making addressing it potentially much more complex. It almost requires a specific plan for each employee. As an example, as care workers master their role, then, for many, expectations of personal and professional development – for example, progressing further on a career pathway – become more important. They will have differing psychological needs and motivations, but there are always improvements that can be made to job quality and culture that benefit all.

Benchmarking and goals

Benchmarking your staff turnover is also not straight-forward. Do you compare your turnover to other care providers in the region (if you can find the relevant information) or by sub-sector, such as homecare? I see different rates depending on ownership structure. For example, not-for-profits and public sector employers usually keep their staff longer than independent providers.

As a rule, providers with a staff turnover of over 50% a year should expect to be able to reduce this by half with a committed and sustained effort. There are diminishing returns when attempting to drive turnover below 20%, although even for exemplar organisations at this level or below, many of the retention techniques we are going to discuss will improve morale and reduce workplace stress.

When you consider the powerful headwinds a care worker experiences against staying in employment, it is remarkable that the sector only has the level of turnover it does. A large part of the reason for this is that many care staff have huge commitment and love for those they care for, so they stay despite compelling reasons to quit. We will look at this important aspect – the reasons why staff stay, rather than the reasons they leave – in Chapter 14. In my experience, this centres around the unique bundle of psychological rewards that those with a caring nature gain from this work.

We must, as a sector, be careful not to exploit this commitment, for example by expecting already over-worked staff to pick up extra shifts because we know they won't say no. As recruitment becomes harder and either existing staff get stretched or less reliable staff join and leave rapidly, the devoted and dependable stalwarts are put upon to cover again and again.

The cost to your organisation

The full financial damage caused by unnecessary frontline care staff loss is rarely measured outside of academic papers (such as Seavey 2004),[56] but it is mind-boggling when you examine it. The most obvious cost is experienced by residential care providers who are forced to call in agency staff to maintain their staffing levels. These can be huge sums, even more so as the labour market has tightened up. Homecare providers use agency staff much less commonly, so it is the loss of revenue by not delivering care that is the easiest to quantify for this sector.

Apart from these hard costs, there are also the extra costs of recruiting and training replacements, but the major organisational damage is in the impact on managers and existing staff. Loyal staff are the ones who suffer most when their colleagues leave. Some new recruits leave the organisation suddenly. Their workload must be picked up at short notice, so resentment and stress build up quickly and morale drops, pushing more staff to quit. In addition, staff see the management as inefficient and poor judges of character, causing a further loss of trust.

The frequent loss of new starters is most often a recruit-ment problem, as we touched on earlier, but can also be caused by a variety of operational factors we will examine later. Whatever the cause, it destabilises the workforce. Leavers are sometimes not complimentary about their experience, damaging your reputation in the local recruitment market. In extreme cases, they bring tribunal claims.

It is not just frontline staff turnover that has an influence. As admin or support staff leave, so their knowledge and relationships with the care workers go too. Replacements probably won't be told who worked all last Christmas to cover staff shortages, so care staff end up feeling a little less appreciated and connected to your organisation.

Societal impacts

The wider cost to society of poor turnover performance is not incurred by the provider. It is, however, by far the biggest negative impact on the quality of care experi-enced by the vulnerable in society, be that feeling rushed by an over-stretched care worker, a lack of dignity from having strangers administer their personal care, or care errors due to fatigue or inexperience. In many cases, families also experience worry, disruption and stress.

Perhaps most damaging is the disorientation caused by the loss of strong relationships built up between consumers and trusted care staff. Care workers who see their clients regularly are able to spot subtle but serious declines in their health early. Frequent staff changes therefore can contribute to more hospitalisations and a greater burden on the healthcare system.

There is a strong argument that a weakened social care sector directly impacts family carers, causing them to leave the workforce to take on caring responsibilities that were previously covered by paid care staff. In the UK and globally, the demand for workers is outstripping supply. Much of this shortage – and the costs to the economy of lost tax revenues and slower growth, or even shrinkage – can be addressed. BCG reported that over half of the country's workers care for children, parents or other adult family members; 43% of those depend on paid care workers – either childcare or aged care – to be able to go to work. They concluded that 'Without a healthy care economy, the workforce falls apart.'[57]

Summary

- Measure and monitor your staff turnover, particularly voluntary staff loss.

- Identify when in the employee lifecycle staff turnover is highest.

- Too many 'good leavers'? Check out my Top 20 Retention Techniques in Chapters 15 and 16.

- However painful your staff turnover feels, it's worse for those your organisation cares for.

13

Why Is Care Work A Revolving Door?

Why do care staff leave? It's a simple enough question to ask, but finding the answers has taken me over twelve years and I am still discovering more about this topic. There are many, many factors. A number are interrelated, and each employer will have their own unique combination of causes. Having said that, I have shaped an approach to help employers frame and understand their likely turnover causes, which I share in this chapter. In the following one, I look at the reasons care workers stay – what keeps them loyal? These are not two sides of the same coin, as you might think. You need to understand both drivers to fully get a grip on improving workforce stability.

You may think the best approach to understanding why your staff leave is to ask them in an exit interview, but it depends on who is asking. Is it the manager they can't stand? Perhaps they can't be bothered to respond. Most exit interview reports have 'personal reasons' as the most common response – could that be masking an underlying cause? It also depends on whether leavers are willing to speak to you at all. Equally, if they were unsuitable for the job or poor performers, are they going to admit that?

Intent to leave versus actually quitting

Your staff turnover percentage is a fact. It is easy to measure and has real consequences. But what it doesn't tell you is how many of your team *intend* to leave. What if a large number of your workforce are disengaged and want to move on, but are unable to do so due to inertia, fear or a lack of alternative employment? We saw this situation during the peak of the Covid-19 pandemic in 2020. Staff turnover dropped across the sector – a complete reversal of a long-term upward trend. Much of that was, it turned out, due to a lack of alternatives during lockdowns and the shutting down of many other employment sectors. We know this because as soon as lockdown ended, turnover rates accelerated rapidly.

So, it is important to monitor employee satisfaction, not just turnover. Even if your employee satisfaction is high, turnover can still be problematic. It has been noted in research by Dill, Morgan and Marshall in 2013[58] that low-wage health workers are at heightened risk of 'push factors' such as personal, family or financial issues that cause a worker to leave their job despite their enjoyment of the work and their intention to stay with their employer.

Switchers or leavers?

In England in 2021, 63% of all those who started a new care role were already care workers moving organisations – what I term 'switchers'. The move may be beneficial to that individual, but it doesn't grow workforce capacity – rather, it creates another vacancy to fill. Those who exit the sector altogether are 'leavers'. If the majority of those leaving you are switchers, it can indicate cultural problems.

Modelling the causes of staff turnover

I have built on existing research from Hollander, Feldman, Sapienza and Kane[59] along with other research to create a causal model, shown below, for the main causes driving care staff to leave. This focuses on controllable factors, so it doesn't fully address inescapable aspects like the demanding nature of the work, nor the unsociable hours or unpleasantness of some facets of personal care, but it can help zero in on issues that you can fix.

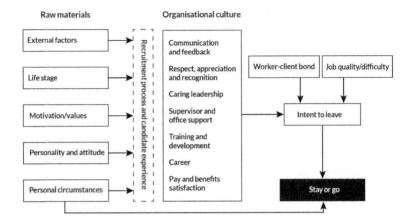

Causal model for why care staff become regrettable leavers

Let's review the main recurring causes. In each case, it is worth noting if these could apply in your situation.

Raw materials

External factors

Social care is buffeted by many external headwinds that are outside the control of employers and can drive significant levels of workforce turnover. There are almost too many examples to pick from, but a few are listed below.

Government policy. For example, the mandatory vaccination requirement in English care homes during Covid-19 saw over 30,000 staff leave their jobs. Brexit was another, much more significant and long-term blow to the sector.

Covid-19 and its impact on burnout and the labour market. The pandemic placed immense strain on the workforce, which was then followed by a significant demand for workers from sectors such as hospitality as lockdowns ended and EU workers failed to return.

Cost of living increases. Sharp increases in energy and food costs can force care workers to seek higher-paid work or take on more hours, which risks stress and burnout. On the flipside, it may bring back into the workforce those who have chosen to be economically inactive, for example those with a modest pension that no longer covers the bills.

The media image of care work. The national media can shape the narrative of care work and the sector does not benefit from the same positive media coverage that the NHS receives in the UK.

Generational attitudes to employment. I regularly meet longstanding managers that bemoan the work ethic of the younger generation. There is no doubt that the loyalty between a worker and their employer has changed. There is much more emphasis on flexibility and our sector is slow to adapt. Covid-19 has created an expectation that there will be the ability to work from home. However, as the US Bureau of Labor has measured, nine out of ten care sector jobs require a physical presence at the point of delivery. This compares to about 20% of professional service jobs.[60]

Life stage

Much of the research into what makes a successful care worker identifies that this type of work, because it is anchored by inter-personal relationships and the caring and compassionate element, requires emotional maturity.[61] That doesn't infer that older care workers are more successful in every single case, but there is a large body of evidence that the young, typically, are not as attracted to adult social care and, if they join, don't stay as long.

There is also a year-on-year decline in the absolute numbers of under-twenty-fives entering social care frontline roles.[62] Part of this decline is down to societal changes and the prevalence of technology, such as social media apps that reduce face-to-face communication skills and encourage insularity.

Motivation/values

There are three main motivations for taking a job as a care worker: the need for work or money; a 'calling' or desire to care; and as a stepping stone to a future career in a related field, such as nursing. Previous research indicates that about a third of care staff see the job as simply a means of earning money. This indicates a large minority of the workforce is here not through choice but necessity. By definition, they will have low job attachment and are primed to leave. By contrast, the importance of having a 'calling' for care cannot be overstated – I explore this area in much more depth in the next chapter.

Personality and attitude

How well an employee's personality and attitude suit the requirements of the job role is an important factor in job performance in any employment sector, but is particularly important in caring roles, since so much of job success is about enjoying the work. In research, when care staff were polled, only 43% said that most of their colleagues exhibited the personality traits of a great care worker,[63] so the sector hasn't yet got this right.

Attitudes, or workplace behaviours. These are also key components. Most involuntary staff turnover is due to poor attitudes, such as unreliability or dishonesty. According to National Care Forum data, in 2016 over 8% of staff turnover was due to dismissals.[64] Voluntary resignations prior to being dismissed will add to this number.

Personal circumstances

Some care workers live chaotic lives. Younger workers in particular have a higher likelihood of personal circumstances that will create conflicts with their employment. These include single parenthood, childcare issues, unreliable transport, financial problems, relationship problems and state benefit restrictions. In many cases, a care worker's family or partner may not be supportive of their work due to the unsociable hours or the fact that they are frequently standing in for extra shifts at short notice. As I mentioned earlier, low pay exacerbates this risk, as the worker is less likely to have a cushion of savings to cope with unexpected costs due to, for example, a car breakdown or childcare costs. More importantly, perhaps, is that those who give emotionally for extended periods hugely benefit from a strong social support infrastructure that can help them decompress and maintain resilience. Not all care workers are lucky enough to have this.

The recruitment process and candidate experience

Poor recruitment

Recruitment plays a major role in determining future staff turnover levels, especially in the first few months of employment. As far back as 1992, before the advent of internet job boards, researchers saw a 24% worsening of tenure when care workers were sourced from newspaper adverts and walk-ins compared to word of mouth and employee referrals.[65] Now, internet job boards deliver an even lower average tenure employee, especially where screening is weak. This can be partly attributed to this source being the go-to place for those needing work rather than having a calling for care. It is too easy to apply without thought or consideration of what a role in frontline care entails.

As the labour market has become much more competitive, so the importance of prioritising values-based recruitment, particularly targeting those in the local community who display the values we seek, regardless of whether they are actively job-seeking, has grown. There are too many alternative and typically better-paying options for those ambivalent to a caring role. We will only succeed in building a stable workforce if we primarily seek those for whom this work uniquely meets their psychological needs.

Ineffective recruitment also impacts existing staff. Unfilled vacancies and the early loss or poor performance of unsuitable new hires increase pressure on those in post to cover. It also, especially for residential care providers, will be a driver of the use of temporary agency staff, which has significant implications for costs and the morale of remaining staff.

Candidate experience

A poor candidate experience mainly causes drop-outs prior to employment, but it can contribute to high staff loss in the first few weeks of employment, principally through unmanaged expectations. There are two examples of this that I see all the time:

1. Existing care staff or those under financial pressure will want to reach their target hours of work per week quickly. If that doesn't happen then they are at high risk of leaving. Similarly, those new to care who are overworked early may drop out due to burnout or exhaustion. It is important to be clear about what their month one earnings are likely to be and try to match that to their needs.

2. Not fully explaining the role, particularly aspects such as personal care and challenging behaviour. As we saw in Chapter 3, ensuring candidates have a clear understanding of all aspects of the role can improve retention by over 20%. This is even more important when you consider how desperately the sector needs to attract those without prior paid care experience – exactly the cohort who benefit most from being prepared for what the job entails.

Organisational culture

Even if you have selected new staff carefully, they can still be driven to leave by the organisation itself in a number of different ways.

Communication and feedback

Frontline staff regularly cite not feeling part of the organisation, not being kept informed or feeling isolated as reasons to leave. With the demands of an increasing workload, managers, coordinators and supervisors have less time to communicate. Covid-19, although devastating for the social care sector, has had the effect of forcing employers to build different communication channels with staff and ensure contact details are kept up to date.

When I toured Australia in 2022, with their equivalent of Skills for Care, we were joined by a well-respected demographer, Bernard Salt AM. He made the fascinating observation that the Australian Government's 'Covid Safe' app (their equivalent of the NHS Covid-19 app) had, at a stroke, familiarised older generations of Australians with how to download an app for the first time. This would have paved the way for far greater uptake of communication platforms such as WhatsApp than would have been the case prior to the pandemic. This would have also been reflected in the older demographic profile of the social care workforce.

Respect, appreciation and recognition

US polls have found that appreciation, informal praise and acknowledgement matter most to care workers. A study by Mittal, Rosen and Leana[66] is just one of several research projects that found a lack of respect was the number one cause of good staff leaving their jobs.

If I could change one aspect of the current social care market, it would be to improve the respect for and appreciation of frontline care staff. This disregard for care workers can come from all quarters: supervisors, office staff, managers, their own families and wider society, but organisational disrespect is within our grasp as providers to fix. In nursing homes, nurses can be guilty of medical 'snobbery' toward care workers. The healthcare profession has a hierarchy where those with more education and qualifications can presume those below them lack expertise. You can also regularly hear unintentional disrespectful language, such as managers referring to staff as 'my girls' or using phrases such as 'all the way down to the care staff'. This is so engrained that care workers commonly refer to themselves as 'just a care worker'.

A lack of recognition is a related challenge. Recognition is the formal crediting of staff achievement or results (where appreciation is usually less formal and focuses on the value of the individual). It can take the form of an award, public acknowledgement or a reward. There is a clear link between workplace recognition and staff morale.

However, attempts at recognition can backfire. A common example is the Employee of the Month. Often, management think this is a positive scheme, but it can be seen by staff as arbitrary and unfair and could be contributing to staff dissatisfaction.

Tip: I will explain how to upgrade your appreciation in Chapter 15.

Caring leadership

The adage that people leave their boss not their job holds doubly true in the caring profession. Those who care for others tend to be sensitive to human relationships and highly empathetic. Therefore, leadership style is likely to have a more profound influence than with other workforces, such as sales teams.

Research by Donoghue and Castle[67] found that nursing homes with autocratic leadership styles had staff turnover four times higher than those with a much more caring, consensus-led approach where decision-making was shared. Disturbingly, across the 2,900 nursing homes they surveyed, nearly 70% of managers did not display this preferred style. We'll look at some simple ways of addressing this in Chapter 15.

Supervisor and office support

Supervisors, the first line of management in most care settings, are also often lacking in interpersonal skills training, such as in conflict resolution and the use of blame-free language. This is a glaring gap in the support provided by the sector, and the value of fixing this is illustrated perfectly by the long-term work of the Para-professional Healthcare Institute (PHI) in New York. PHI demonstrated huge improvements in retention by supporting supervisors in these areas, as we will see later. Support extends to a willingness for management to be flexible and sympathetic when frontline staff get hit with 'life shocks', such as a late childcare cancellation or transport failures, but also to recognise care workers need time to top up their 'emotional bank accounts' or risk compassion fatigue, burnout and overwhelm.

Training and development

Training is critical for a care worker's confidence and feeling of self-development. Skills for Care measured a 9.5% lower staff turnover rate amongst care workers who had received some form of training compared to those that hadn't. Also, investment by the employer in more training continues to pay dividends. Average turnover rates dropped 9.1 percentage points for those with more than thirty instances of training recorded compared to just one instance – most likely induction training.[68] In the UK, induction training is generally of a high standard, particularly in terms of course content. There has been a move towards e-learning, which research shows is a weaker method of learning for frontline care roles and can be more driven by financial reasons than good practice. The most successful method of ensuring competence is on-the-job training wherever possible, but tailoring the learning method as much as possible to the individual's preferred way to learn is the goal.

Career

The need to offer meaningful career pathways is an ongoing challenge for a fragmented industry with a flat organisational structure. Career reasons are cited by over 20% of leavers in surveys,[69] although older workers can place more value on self-development as care practitioners rather than being promoted away from a hands-on care role.

Pay and benefits satisfaction

Pay is a complex area and there is no doubt care workers are underpaid for both the demands of the job and its contribution to society.

The value of pay/benefits satisfaction is not only to contribute to a fair society where the frail and vulnerable have access to the quality care and support they need, but also to allow many workers (the majority female) with unpaid care responsibilities to participate in the workforce for the benefit of the economy. This is increasingly critical as birth rates slow and immigration is restricted.

Improving pay certainly has a large influence on the attractiveness of the job, but surprisingly less so when we're considering what drives people to leave frontline care.[70] The rate of pay and the hours available will matter much more to a worker who is a primary breadwinner with a family to feed than to a retiree with other sources of income, as will the uncertainty of the hours they will receive. Of course, in many cases, there is a cap on what staff can be paid because the state sets the fee rates paid to providers. The ability to guarantee a worker a minimum number of hours of work each week is cited as an important step forward, but when homecare workers on zero hours contracts (no guaranteed work at all) were offered the option of guaranteed hours, only 24% took it up.[71] This was despite evidence to show a higher staff turnover with those on a zero hours contract than those not.[72]

For a further discussion on pay in social care, see Appendix 1.

Worker–client bond

The relationship between the care worker and the person they care for is usually one of the most powerful reasons preventing staff leaving. Many academic research papers, such as a 2019 PhD study[73] looking at the common drivers of retention funded by Cohesion Recruitment, conclude that the key drivers of retention are the clients themselves and the contact time with them. We will explore this in detail in the next chapter, so why are we considering it here? In cases where there is a racial or cultural difference between the worker and the client, these bonds can be weaker, and the minority worker serving a (usually) white client can face racism, which many employers struggle to manage. As the demand for care increases, so we will become more reliant on a diverse workforce to service those needs, creating a greater likelihood of staff experiencing prejudice.

Job quality/difficulty

Care work is tough, both emotionally and physically, but there are characteristics of specific job roles, for example the likelihood of physical attacks by clients, the quality of the rostering or the level of responsibility, that make the experience of doing the job better or worse. Employers have a considerable level of control over the perceived job role quality.

Tip: Watch my two-part whiteboard video series 'Why Do Care Workers Leave You? – Part 1 and 2' at www.savingsocialcare.com/videos

Summary

- There are likely to be many factors behind your staff loss statistics.

- The quality of your recruitment sets the trajectory for later staff turnover.

- A lack of appreciation is the single biggest controllable reason why staff leave.

- Pay is important, but increasing pay alone is not a panacea. It is certainly deserved and long overdue, however. How satisfied staff are with pay is much more important than the actual amount.

14

What Keeps Care Workers In Their Jobs?

Now we have considered many of the reasons why a care worker would leave, it is time to take a more upbeat look at why a huge number of care workers love their jobs, would never consider doing anything else and report high levels of job satisfaction. Within this chapter are the secrets to building a stable and loyal workforce for the future.

I would caution that, in my view, there is a high risk of society, government and employers grossly undervaluing – and in some cases exploiting – care workers because of these characteristics. Depressed pay rates being a prime example.

Who would you love to clone?

For four years, between about 2015 and 2019, I ran regular recruitment and retention workshops for managers across the UK. This was an opportunity to get together and learn new approaches to finding and keeping care staff. As always, the most valuable part of the day was learning from each other and the realisation for attendees that much of what they were doing was, in fact, already best practice. They just never knew.

Social care in the UK has many advantages due to being mostly a large collection of small independent operations – it makes the sector lean, nimble and responsive. A big disadvantage of this, though, is that businesses see each other, especially locally, as competitors. They don't share good practices; they spend too little time engaging with the outside world; and they don't take advantage of the resources and support available.

Equally, it is difficult for researchers to interact with care workers, spread as they are across numerous small companies and in many cases, not being centrally registered, as is the case with many healthcare professions.

So, I decided to undertake some longitudinal, somewhat unscientific qualitative research, focused on answering one question: 'Is there a pattern or repeatable characteristic across the highest-performing frontline care workers in a diverse range of organisations?'

I asked all the attendees of my workshops to commit to some advance homework: they should identify one care worker in their team they would love to clone and ask them what triggered their decision to become a care worker. Is there a common experience we can use to identify others? I also asked which recruitment channel they were sourced through, which I'll come to later. Here are the results:

High performers: what was the trigger for you to become a care worker?

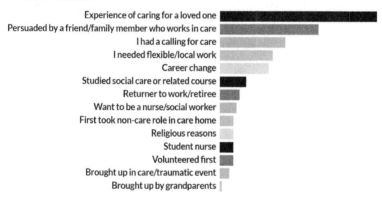

Source: Neil Eastwood's recruitment masterclasses 2015-2019 N=287

This is a profoundly powerful chart because it tells us the secrets to sourcing a loyal, high-performing workforce. Many of you reading this will identify your own reason for being in the sector on the list. Mine is there: religious reasons – I was brought up in a vicarage. Anyway, here is what I conclude:

1. We need a national programme to engage and support those who have had informal caring responsibilities to join the sector (I am thinking about caring for a loved one rather than childcare, unless that child had additional needs).

2. Many care workers would probably have never taken the job had they not been persuaded by a trusted source, like a friend or family member. This means that some wonderful care workers would not have had the self-confidence to apply for the job. This is why enlisting the current workforce to spread the word through employee referral schemes and outreach programmes like *I Care… Ambassadors* (see Appendix 2) is so important.

3. Emotional maturity is a consistent theme: through caring for a loved one, volunteering or experiencing a trauma or loss.

4. The primary driver of simply needing local work is not enough to justify an over-reliance on internet job boards, which mostly trade in this sole characteristic. I would suggest people displaying most of the other characteristics are generally not actively seeing work – certainly not in social care.

What is unique about care work?

To the passer-by in the street, or a job seeker looking for local work, care work is low down on the list and, for those that do consider it, very few actually go on to apply. Research undertaken by the Department of Health and Social Care in 2018 found that amongst adults aged twenty to fifty-five, 24% said they had considered the sector but only one in twenty-five went on to apply.[74] So, why do hundreds of thousands of people in England – and around the world – stick with the role when there are many more well paid and less demanding alternatives?

Care work, unlike most other jobs, is first and foremost 'emotional labour'. A large part of the role requires the worker to manage their own emotions while putting others' emotional and physical needs first. In many cases, that person – the client or resident – is in pain, distress or is unable to have an acceptable quality of life without the intervention of the care worker. Unlike much of healthcare, these needs are not sudden and short-term, but require long-term support, most commonly over years.

In order to stick at this type of work and gain satisfaction from it every day, the requirements of the job must deliver strong intrinsic rewards to the individual doing it, not unlike love. This does not include pay, since that does not compensate for the demands of the job, nor would a much higher rate of pay somehow create the psychological reward to retain those who don't enjoy the work. Pay is an extrinsic reward, a hygiene factor, not a motivational one here. Improving pay is essential but alone it is not enough to build a loyal, caring workforce. So, what 'invisible forces' are at play?

The hidden psychological pull of care work

My favourite explanation of what is happening, unseen, every day to prevent a mass exodus of care workers, is based on research undertaken by Mittal, Rosen and Leana in 2009.[75] I'm going to summarise a version of their findings below.

They argued that turnover can be reduced by addressing factors to do with job dissatisfaction, such as low pay, poor supervision and poor working conditions. But, as important though those may be, these factors are not the same as those that drive motivation to stay. Do we spend too much time focused on trying to prevent staff leaving and not enough on strengthening the reasons for them to stay? Are we missing a deeper understanding of the inherent value of the work? This is not to say we can stop calls for increased pay because care workers with the right values are sufficiently rewarded with a deep sense of fulfilment; rather, we must nurture these factors alongside improved pay and job quality.

Mittal et al argued that there were a number of distinct psychological needs being met for many care workers who reported high job satisfaction, despite poor working conditions. I have picked my top five, influenced by their original work. These are not all experienced by every care worker, but many care workers experience more than one – and perhaps others not included here (in my selected reverse order):

- **A haven from personal challenges.** Many care workers describe their home lives as a challenge. Given their compassionate nature, they may well be caring for others (over half of care workers have family caring responsibilities), they are likely to be under financial constraints and could be managing relationship conflicts, loneliness or health issues. As a result, the familial nature of care can be experienced as something of a reprieve.

- **A commitment to their clients.** The nature of the relationship between a care worker and their client means there is a strong sense of personal responsibility for their welfare. This can manifest itself as additional unpaid contact time or the purchase of gifts from personal finances. It can be almost too traumatic for a care worker to contemplate abandoning 'their' client by leaving the job and so low pay and poor conditions are tolerated for far longer than might be the case in other job roles. Care workers can see themselves as the best advocate for their clients, especially where there are no family members fulfilling that role.

- **Surrogate family.** The deep, personal and long-term nature of the relationship between care workers and their clients can be seen by the worker as like having a surrogate family. In some cases, this can be a particularly powerful bond where, for example, the worker has lost a family member, was brought up in care themselves or their own children have grown up and left home.

- **Emotional satisfaction and pride.** Strong feelings of contribution, accomplishment and self-esteem, mostly generated by gratitude from the client themselves, often less so from managers, is a major retention factor cited by staff. Knowing the impact they are having on the lives of those they support can provide immense personal fulfilment.

- **Religious or spiritual 'calling to care'.** A rarely considered motivation, but one that I think is perhaps the strongest of all, is the deeply held convictions and beliefs of many in the workforce. Since this aspect is rarely spoken about and is mostly an intensely private thing, certainly in an employment context, it goes unresearched and unmeasured. But when you consider the proximity that care work has to mortality, suffering, loss and hope, and how faith can help care workers deal with adversity, I believe it to be one of the most powerful explanations of why our social care system did not collapse many years ago.

Protecting a workforce dependent on emotional labour

Emotional work is largely invisible, unlike physical work. It can also wrongly be seen as 'women's work', 'low value' and 'unskilled'. It has long been under-valued, but is in fact incredibly valuable and requires great strength of character and maturity to deliver well. Emotional labourers risk burnout, compassion fatigue and 'vicarious' stress from seeing others in pain and distress daily. Profound loss and grief are often part of the job but, in most cases, care workers are expected to continue working.

Employers must recognise this unseen 'cost of caring' and ensure more time is given to decompress, grieve and reflect. In the coming chapters, I will suggest simple actions to help ensure care workers' 'emotional cups' are regularly topped up and that we as a sector don't ever lose sight of this overlooked but core aspect of what keeps care workers in their jobs.

Summary

- The top three reasons for becoming a care worker for high performers are family care experience, being persuaded by a family member or friend and having a 'calling' to care.

- Care work is emotional labour and hygiene factors, such as pay, however important, do not address this aspect.

- There is a spiritual or even religious aspect to caring for many, as well as strong bonds between a care worker and their clients, which we must understand and nurture to be better employers.

15
Keeping Staff –
Ten Quick Wins

In this chapter, I pick out my favourite quick win staff-retention methods. Based on my research, they are, to varying degrees, easy to implement and deliver positive results in care businesses around the world.

They are:

- Welcome programme

- Inviting good leavers back

- Letters home

- Regular appreciation from a supervisor

- Increased client–worker bond

- Better recruitment

- Friday phone calls or one-to-ones

- Recognition programmes

- Technology

- Improving leadership styles

Welcome programme

A simple welcome card, signed by all the office staff and posted to the home of the new employee as soon as they accept your offer of employment, is a small but powerful message that they are valued. But this should be part of a coordinated welcome programme that swings into action each time a new starter accepts your job offer. Here are some simple but effective ways of doing that:

- **Put up a welcome sign in reception with the new employee's name on.** People love seeing their name mentioned and this instantly reassures the new starter that they matter, are expected and are in the right building.

- **Make the day fun.** If the first day is mostly made up of induction training, then why not put up balloons and lay on cakes? These will be particularly valuable if you have baked them yourself.

- **Say, 'Hello.'** The care manager should introduce the training if they are not leading it themselves and explain how important the new staff are to the company.

- **Pass around a photo.** If possible, before the employee's first day, show office staff their photo (taken as part of the application process) and give their name. Ask staff to memorise the face, so that when the new starter is in the kitchen making a drink, they are greeted by name.

- **Hands-on training.** If the first day is mostly classroom training, try to include some practical elements and, if possible, get new staff to meet future colleagues and those they will be caring for.

- **A 'goody bag'** on completion of the new starter's training is a nice touch. This could include foot lotion (aching feet is a common complaint from those new to care) and other useful small items, such as torches for community-based roles. Branded workwear is also popular, such as fleeces.

- **VIP treatment.** in a LinkedIn conversation, Leigh Davis, a leading US-based expert in this area, suggested to me reserving a parking space for each new starter on their first day with a board with their name on, marked 'Reserved'. What a lovely touch.

- **Social events.** Although arranging regular social events is important for long-term retention, creating an environment where new starters can meet the wider team and managers in a relaxed setting should be high on your list.

 Tip: Buy a bulk pack of welcome cards and get office staff to sign many at once. Keep the same pen to add each new starter's name, and they are ready to send each time you need them.

 Tip: Agree what you will include in your welcome programme and ensure a member of staff is responsible for ensuring it happens.

Inviting good leavers back

We've learned that good leavers can be persuaded to return in up to three out of ten cases. If you haven't already got a good leaver scheme in place, then go back over all the leavers in the past year and agree with the manager which ones you'd be happy to re-employ. Then contact them with the offer to return. This is most powerful if those they cared for ask about them or you have some positive change or news to share. Start by sending a 'We miss you' postcard and follow up with a text message.

Letters home

An influential and usually forgotten stakeholder in the decision of a care worker to stay or leave your organisation is the spouse or partner at home. Partners do not always experience or value the intrinsic rewards of caring for another person. This can make them adopt a negative attitude to their partner's employer or to social care in general. As a result, they become strong influencers in a stay or leave decision.

Find ways to involve an employee's family with the company or communicate how much their partner is valued. The easiest method is to write a personal note of thanks home at least once a year, not simply at Christmas when this might be expected. It's better done when you have a specific example of good practice to praise or at random times, and is particularly effective when the most senior member of staff you can find signs the letter.

 Tip: Watch my video on the importance of relationships at www.savingsocialcare.com/videos

Regular appreciation from a supervisor

We know from multiple studies going back to the 1980s that appreciation is what care workers value the most.[76] And it costs absolutely nothing to give.

If that is the case, why have we not all baked this into our management approach long ago? Well, before we get to that, let's back up and define 'appreciation', because it is often confused with its close relative 'recognition'. Appreciation is the informal acknowledgement of the value or contribution of an individual. In this case, it comes from the line manager of the employee.

There are several reasons why this has not been prioritised by employers. It's partly the high turnover in social care, which means organisations have a short 'memory', partly because the sector is fragmented and sharing of best practice is weak, and partly due to poor supervisor support. But it's mainly because supervisors and managers are under continuous pressure. When time is short or priorities are urgent, then taking a minute to say, 'Well done' is the first casualty.

Good care workers desperately need regular affirmation – they do a demanding, emotionally and physically draining job for low pay and scant respect from society. Appreciation is oxygen for them. Usually, they will get gratitude from those they care for, but it has extra significance when it comes from their line manager.

So how can you institutionalise regular appreciation from managers and supervisors? Here are two proven methods:

1. **The praise rule.** Karl Pillemer[77] recommends instituting a rule that all supervisors look for and publicly praise at least one example of good care from their team every day, then write it down and record it in their personnel file. The objective here is to get supervisors to positively reinforce good behaviour instead of berating staff for mistakes.

2. **Add reminders** to your work calendar at random times over the next few weeks, each one triggering you to call in a member of your team to deliver some positive feedback. It is important not to include any criticism or reminders in this session – it should be purely for communicating that they are valued. Cite specific behaviour where possible, which is best garnered from their clients or residents, or family members.

 Tip: Set up a system to solicit praise from those being cared for to feed your appreciation engine.

Increased client–worker bond

As we learned earlier, the connection between a consumer and their care worker is usually the primary reason for staff remaining in the job. Employers can intervene to strengthen these bonds by increasing the 'being with' compared to the 'doing to' contact time, but there is a way of speeding up the building of this bond when client and worker first meet.

Learn as much as you can about each consumer. Not just their care needs and preferences, but their history, interests, hobbies, past life and how long they have lived in the area. Next, make the same enquiry with new starters. How long have they lived in the area? What are their connections with it? What interests do they have? Find things that the consumer and the worker have in common and brief the new care worker before their first meeting with their client. This helps overcome any awkwardness and speed up the formation of a deeper relationship.

 Tip: Watch my whiteboard video 'The Importance of Relationships' explaining this at www.savingsocial-care.com/videos

Better recruitment

This topic formed most of the earlier part of this book, so I am not going to go into detail here, only to reiterate that finding the right staff is the single biggest impact you can have on both performance in the job and how long they stay.

Is good recruitment in any way 'easy'? Well, not really, but neither is poor recruitment. In fact, processing unreliable, half-hearted applicants, suffering no-shows, drop-outs and managing bad staff out of the business is much harder than good recruitment.

 Tip: Look at your sources of staff, measure conversion rates and ensure your pre-screening is robust.

Friday phone calls or one-to-ones

Stephen Tweed, who has great experience of effective retention techniques in the US homecare and home health sectors, recommends[78] that managers set aside time at the end of the week to call frontline staff individually to check in and ask if they have any concerns. In a residential setting, it is much easier to reach those staff on shift by simply walking around the building. It requires more effort in a dispersed community-based organisation.

Recognition programmes

In a sector with a flat pay rate and limited scope for meaningful pay rises, visible rewards and status symbols take on extra significance. Research into the use of these in the care sector in the US from as far back as 1990[79] has found that they were extremely important to participants. The forms of recognition studied included bonuses, different uniforms and pin badges, and were given as a reward for length of service, reliability (for example a 90% attendance across the year), taking on more responsibility, such as being a peer mentor, or for acquiring specialist skills, like becoming a dementia care practitioner.

Given the sector's ongoing challenges with reliability and staff absence, an incentive for attendance over a defined period should be effective if implemented well (see Chapter 16 – Performance-related Pay for more on this). Ask staff what methods of recognition they would value. Consider which behaviours are most important for your organisation to reward. Don't make any recognition too complex or unattainable – simple coloured pin badges can be purchased cheaply from online education sector suppliers, for example.

 Tip: Be cautious about using familiar bronze, silver and gold colours for lapel pins as consumers might ask why they are not assigned a 'gold' care worker.

Technology

Technology offers new possibilities each year for social care providers. One of the challenges for employers is that there seems to be a confusing array of competing possibilities, most requiring an investment of time to consider and pilot. Some can also come at a considerable cost, although the rise of pay-as-you-go cloud-based software has largely removed upfront capital outlays. Others can be quick, cheap and deliver a big benefit instantly.

Technology can now help staff retention in several ways, such as:

- Improving care worker efficiency, for example removing the need for form-filling and thereby reducing boredom and increasing contact time with consumers.

- Reducing the risk of errors with medication recording smartphone applications, which can lower care worker stress.

- Pre-screening for behaviour and job fit, so candidates who are unsuitable are screened out before being hired.

- Making staff feel involved and increasing a sense of family, for example by creating WhatsApp groups for care teams to keep in touch, share tips and introduce a sense of fun.

We must be careful that the introduction of technology doesn't replace communication between the office and staff, particularly for field-based workers, otherwise it may increase feelings of isolation or be seen as a way of spying on staff. Overall, though, new technology presents big opportunities to support employers to select better staff and improve the work lives of care workers.

 Tip: You'll probably be cold-called by sector technology salespeople on a regular basis. I find attending care trade shows or asking for advice from others on LinkedIn groups are good ways of finding out what technology is seeing rapid adoption.

Improving leadership styles

A study by Donoghue and Castle in 2009, as mentioned in Chapter 13, found a clear link between the style of leadership in nursing homes in the US and the rate of staff turnover of both nurses and care assistants.[80] When leaders were mapped against known styles of leadership with all other variables constant, the study found that the most autocratic style was associated with frontline staff leaving at a rate of almost four times that of settings with the most collaborative style. The study also discovered almost 70% of nursing home leaders did not display this 'consensus' style. Fortunately, the authors of the study noted it is possible to change your leadership style over time, which presents an opportunity for those managers willing to change.

Although it is not easy to acknowledge that you need to change and effect a long-term shift in your leadership style, there are baby steps that you can take to see improvements. These include regularly asking staff, 'What should we do in this situation?', recognising you are not always right and, where possible, listening first rather than reacting with your initial thought.

 Tip: Michael West's book *Compassionate Leadership*[81] is an excellent guide.

Summary

- There are a range of retention methods that can be executed quickly. If I had to choose one, it would be to improve the level of supervisory appreciation of staff.

16
Keeping Staff – Ten Long-term Improvements

Most retention interventions are not quick fixes. They require either time, money, effort, personnel changes, employee engagement or wholesale cultural change. It is beyond the scope of this book to provide detailed implementation plans for the ten methods I am introducing here, but I have signposted resources where possible.

My ten recommended long-term retention projects are:

1. Peer mentoring

2. Coaching Supervision

3. Career matrix

4. Increased contact time

5. Interpersonal skills training

6. Cultural competence

7. Maturing your workforce

8. Supportive work culture

9. Performance-related pay

10. Shared decision-making

Peer mentoring

Two common causes of new starters leaving is a feeling of isolation and a lack of confidence. This is especially true where staff turnover in the first few weeks of employment is high, because this unnerves the employee further. It is also likely that existing staff will 'hold back' from getting to know the new starter since they don't expect them to be around for long.

Supervisors perform an important role in supporting new staff, but the relationship is such that care workers can feel reluctant to ask for advice or share that they may benefit from emotional support. This is where a peer-mentoring programme comes in. The concept is to assign each new starter a 'buddy' or mentor who is doing the same job as them but is experienced in the role and can answer questions, give advice and provide emotional support as required.

Peer-mentoring programmes have delivered impressive improvements in staff retention when operated effectively. Results[82] have included a doubling of staff retention in homecare operations and the elimination of agency staff within six months of implementation in a residential care setting. An extra benefit of operating a peer-mentoring programme is that it provides an opportunity for personal development for care workers with longer service, who perhaps aren't keen on or suitable for formal supervisory roles.

This all sounds compelling but, like most things worth having, it does require some planning, commitment, communication and persistence. The following are tips from US researchers and providers who have introduced and tested peer mentoring in social care.

- **Mentor selection** should have an element of self-nomination as the role requires commitment on top of other duties. At least one year of experience in the role is recommended. Not every individual will have the right personality to be a success.

- **Mentor training** is a critical part of every successful scheme. Typically, training lasts at least three days and covers problem-solving, coaching skills, leadership, motivation techniques and effective communication skills.

- **Mentor assignment** should be limited to no more than three mentees, so one or two is probably the best arrangement.

- **Mentor roles and responsibilities** should not undermine the supervisor and are usually restricted to answering questions, giving advice and providing support and encouragement during stressful periods for the new starter.

- **Mentor remuneration** can work best as a bonus for each successful mentorship (usually six months). In some cases, a mobile phone is provided by the company to recognise the extra communication required by this role.

The Paraprofessional Healthcare Institute (PHI)[83] has led the way on providing employers with practical and tested guidance on implementing peer-mentoring schemes.

 Tip: As a starting point, take a look at PHI's paper introducing the concept in practical accessible language.[84]

Coaching Supervision

A care worker's primary organisational connection is with their supervisor. This can frequently be a fraught relationship and is often cited as the cause of a care worker leaving their job. Staff, particularly new starters, are trying to cope with the physical and emotional demands of their job, often with an unstable or complex personal situation. If the employee is the primary breadwinner, then they will likely have limited resources to cope with sudden crises such as a failure in childcare, transport or unplanned debt. Equally, supervisors can be given the role without enough training and support, particularly in how to avoid blaming or coming across as scolding care staff.

The PHI has for many years researched a novel method of enhancing this relationship between care worker and supervisor, called Coaching Supervision, which focuses on giving the supervisor the ability to help frontline staff to develop problem-solving skills to prioritise and manage their relationships both in work and outside.[85] The results of these interventions have been dramatic and prevented otherwise high-performing staff from leaving the workforce unnecessarily.

The PHI has also produced an excellent free guide[86], which I thoroughly recommend reading if you'd like to learn more. It has further paid training resources to help launch a similar programme on its website (US-focused).

Career matrix

Offering a meaningful career to frontline care workers has been a vexing subject for many years. Younger workers tend to place a higher priority on career advancement than older workers. In fact, emphasising the career opportunities in your organisation can be a turn-off to older workers.

There is a common misconception that career development must mean being promoted away from hands-on work with consumers. There are at least five alternative career pathways for care workers, which are much less often considered. These are:

- Specialisms – training to become a practitioner in one or more aspects of care, for example dementia or challenging behaviour

- Peer mentoring – learning and using interpersonal communication skills to support inexperienced colleagues through the first few months of their employment

- Achieving higher 'grades' of care worker reflecting experience and tenure

- Supporting the recruitment process by interviewing candidates

- Becoming an *I Care… Ambassador* (see Appendix 2) or community outreach champion

These options help overcome job monotony and dissatisfaction with a lack of recognition, and keep staff on the frontline for longer, where they are happiest. In a long-term test in the US homecare sector where a new grade of care worker was created to reward experienced staff, annual retention for this group rose from 52% in 2006 to 90% in 2009[87] (although other interventions were also launched at the time). Certainly, having 'experts' in your team does wonders for your wider reputation.

Think about the different options for career development as described above and consider if these are available to your frontline staff. Have you asked them how they would like to develop their career or are you making assumptions?

 Tip: Watch my whiteboard video 'Career options in frontline care' at www.savingsocialcare.com/videos for more on this topic.

Increased contact time

There is a clear and proven link between contact time and the quality of care experienced by the consumer, measured in many studies.[88] As contact time is squeezed, as we saw particularly during Covid-19, so we see increases in hospital admissions for avoidable conditions, such as urinary tract infections (the leading cause of acute conditions that should not normally require hospital admission in elderly patients).

There is a strong link between the quality of care delivered and staff turnover. If staff are rushed, they are not only prone to making mistakes or missing health changes in those they care for, but also to becoming demoralised and frustrated. Increasing contact time is hard to achieve since, in many cases, there is not the funding to allow it, but by taking the pressure off staff and incorporating some 'being with' time, you could offset any extra costs with the reduced risk of losing a valuable member of staff and the disruption of recruiting to replace them. Some community-based businesses arrange coffee mornings for their customers and find staff volunteer to help so they can spend some more time with those they care for.

Interpersonal skills training

Relationships are at the heart of social care, but most training focuses on 'hard skills' such as moving and handling, medication administration and first aid.

Training in softer skills such as problem-solving, negotiation, conflict resolution and stress management can help employees manage the demands of the job much better, reduce turnover and make them feel valued. It also helps them in their personal life. Ongoing training programmes also give staff an opportunity to get to know each other. Just the process of meeting regularly in small groups can foster supportive relationships amongst attendees.

There has been a steady move toward delivering some training as e-learning (digitally delivered training content), which offers flexibility and practicality where, for example, there is only one person to be trained, making classroom delivery too costly.

Although e-learning has a role, where possible it is best for new starters to engage and discuss with others as they learn. Be cautious about removing the human element at this critical early stage of employment. Consider implementing at least one ongoing supportive relationship-focused training course, prioritising interactive face-to-face and collaborative teaching methods over e-learning or classroom styles of delivery to maximise the development of relationships.

Cultural competence

The density of migrants in the care workforce varies widely. In the UK, it is most concentrated in London, where a high percentage of the workforce was born outside the UK, while in other areas this concentration is diluted – approximately 10% of the workforce in the south, dropping to a few percent in northern England.[89]

Being from a different culture presents challenges to the care worker, and to those they care for. Research found that minority workers had lower levels of job satisfaction,[90] and that managers underestimated the cultural problems more than frontline workers. While poor levels of English was one of the main causes of a lack of tolerance from colleagues, consumers and their families, non-verbal behaviour was also an issue.

It is therefore important to work toward developing a 'culturally competent' workplace to minimise poor job satisfaction, racism and confusion caused by a lack of understanding of other cultures. Levels of acceptance and job satisfaction of minority workers have been improved by their employer offering English lessons and providing awareness training to colleagues, consumers and their families on cultural differences, including religious practices, food, music and end-of-life customs.

If you think that your organisation could benefit from a cultural competence approach, a good starting point is the Mather Lifeways Cultural Competence checklists, which help organisations identify strengths and weaknesses in their current approach.[91]

Maturing your workforce

While it is vital that younger people are encouraged to join the care workforce, there is overwhelming evidence that older workers stay longer and perform better in the job, particularly in community care roles.[92] A recruitment strategy that over-relies on internet job boards, social media and sources where those actively seeking work gather will be biased toward younger job seekers. Employers must have a viable strategy to target and attract older workers too.

Why are older workers more successful in the role? There are multiple reasons, such as more life experience and therefore more empathy, greater emotional maturity, better temperament, lower job mobility and expectations, greater reliability and lower financial needs. Develop a recruitment strategy and messaging that appeals to older people and target places in the community where they gather, as described in Chapter 10.

 Tip: Ensure your recruitment process is not discriminatory. James Sage, Employment Partner in RWK Goodman LLP and Head of Health and Social Care, has provided some guidance in Appendix 3.

Supportive work culture

If you walk into any care home or homecare office, it quickly becomes apparent when staff feel supported and valued, as there is a happy atmosphere. Social care can become too much about crisis, blame, pressure and stress. Employers must work hard to counterbalance these forces and create an atmosphere of support.

This can partly be achieved by introducing the formal techniques we have considered so far, including coaching supervision and peer mentoring, but there are many smaller and less structured actions that contribute to shifting the culture of an organisation in a positive direction. Here are a few examples.

Introduce regular informal meetings to allow frontline staff to discuss challenges and share experiences, focusing on the group solving the challenges rather than being management-led information downloads. By regular, I mean perhaps monthly, and attendees should be paid for their time and travel if applicable.

Offer staff emotional support services, for example from an outside organisation, or some time for reflection to deal with the loss of a client or resident. Staff can be more willing to open up about their wellbeing challenges if the manager first shares their own struggles.

Encourage office-based and administrative staff to experience hands-on care so they can appreciate the demands facing a care worker. Where possible, office staff should attend the induction training sessions that new starters undergo.

Set up WhatsApp groups for staff teams so they can communicate with and support each other. These require regular curating to ensure they are being used appropriately.

Organise regular social events so staff can interact without the pressures of work.

Performance-related pay

Using discretionary pay awards to incentivise good workplace behaviours is not uncommon in other sectors, but rare in social care where I have only come across a few cases. The behaviour most targeted for improvement is absence. In other low-wage sectors, small financial rewards paid after a period of low or no absence have reduced absence by as much as half.

One care home in Oxfordshire has operated a discretionary pay award for over twenty years, with great success. The Managing Partner explained:

> 'All care and domestic staff qualify for an extra 60p bonus for every hour that they work, provided they come to every shift they have agreed to work over a four-week period. If they miss a single shift over the four-week period then they lose their bonus for the whole of the four-week period. 75% of staff get their bonuses at the end of the four-week period. This means that management can be quite confident that the home will be well staffed all the time. To avoid any arguments, there are virtually no exceptions granted for non-attendance. Staff are either at work, or they are not. Another home that operated this system for many years thought their staff had become so reliable that they no longer needed their bonus scheme. However, after stopping it their staff attendance became erratic and they re-introduced the bonus scheme. You must commit to this for the long-term.'

Although every example I have come across so far has been positive, there is little widespread evidence to draw on, so this is an area for further study and piloting for employers with high levels of absence, after suitable legal advice. If you are struggling with high levels of unauthorised absence, even a small payment can change behaviour based on similar workforces in other sectors. Some employers may be uncomfortable rewarding staff for just turning up, which is an understandable view, but this may deliver a noticeable improvement to care delivery.

The Care Friends app offers a feature where managers can award 'bonus points' instantly to recognise good work, an accomplishment or as an incentive to pick up a dropped shift. This has become a popular method of recognising and rewarding staff. Over £1 million in points has been earned this way by care workers to date. This has brought the concept of performance-related bonuses to a much wider audience.

Shared decision-making

In a poll of care workers, 47% said they were dissatisfied due to having too little say in the care of consumers.[93] In fact, employers often forget that care workers usually have more contact time than anyone else with those they care for and so are best placed to anticipate their needs or spot a change in their health or mobility. Too often, their views are ignored.

Find ways to seek the care workers' input into client reviews and operational changes that will affect them. Why not ask care workers to interview candidates, provide feedback on supervisors or give tours to prospective residents and their families?

Summary

- While each of these longer-term interventions has been successful, do not attempt to implement too much in one go. Pick the ones that you think could address specific staffing issues in your organisation and research the best way to deliver these for your circumstances.

17
What Next?

This book cannot prescribe a tailored action plan for your exact recruitment or retention situation, as it necessarily covers many different types of care provision across a wide range of locations. But it does provide an overview of the major factors and components of recruitment and retention of care workers for you to consider, together with tips and techniques that you can adapt and test. If, after reading this, you are up for refreshing the way you find and keep care workers, here are the steps you need to take:

- **Perform a recruitment audit.** This sounds a bit daunting, but it doesn't have to be. The first step is to see what data you can get your hands on to set a benchmark for your current performance. I talked about the numbers I look for when auditing a care provider in Chapter 4. These figures will likely shine a spotlight on outliers you need to address as a priority. You might prefer to seek external help, as an alternative.

- **Map your turnover.** When is it worst? Talk to staff to find out.

- **Develop a realistic plan.** We can get over-ambitious about overhauling the way we recruit or introducing new methods of stemming staff loss. Stephen Tweed, a US expert in social care strategy, warns we must have a focused recruiting or retention system that we can repeat every week.

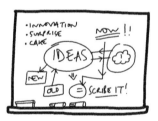

- For recruiters, he recommends they follow the 'Rule of Three'. He explained this to me as, 'Picking just three categories of recruiting and developing a system to use these techniques every week. Test your ads. Improve your application process. Refine your selection system. And keep recruiting every week'.

- **Clear ownership and buy-in.** If you are a recruiter or responsible for staff retention, then it is essential to get buy-in from senior management before launching any of the recommendations that require high-level support. Equally, if you are an owner or senior manager, then do not attempt to implement any of these changes without first ensuring that someone takes responsibility for owning them.

- If I could identify one characteristic of care providers who have got maximum benefit from what we've discussed in this book, it would be those who are great implementers.

- **Measure, test, adjust, repeat.** Care workers, both in post and prospective, are human and exposed to many competing pressures, as well as each being unique individuals. Changing your methods of recruiting, on-boarding and engaging them will require trial and error. Small regular improvements will soon build up, and looking back at the way things were after just a few months can be enormously rewarding.

- **Don't put it off.** It's easy to put off any changes because you are too busy. The old adage 'We're too busy chasing chickens to mend the fence' could not be truer in almost every social care operation. Focus on the fence.

I wish you every success with your recruitment and retention in the coming years.

Neil Eastwood,
Richmond, London
March 2023

Further Reading

If you'd like to learn more about this topic, I strongly recommend four books as must-reads for any social care workforce practitioner:

- Mel Kleiman's *Hire Tough, Manage Easy: How to find and hire the best hourly employees* (Humetrics Press, 2006)

- Stephen Tweed's *Conquering the Crisis: Strategies for Caregiver Recruiting and Retention* (Red Letter Press, 2017), available from www.conqueringthecrisis.com

- Leigh Davis's *3 Simple Steps to Getting MORE Applicants*, e-book available at www.davisdelaney.com.

- Michael West's *Compassionate Leadership: Sustaining wisdom, humanity and presence in health and social care* (The Swirling Leaf Press, 2021)

Additional Resources

If you are based in the UK, then Skills for Care and the Social Care Institute for Excellence are highly recommended sources of support and ideas, as well as the many regional organisations and associations that work tirelessly for the sector on many operational aspects, including recruitment and retention:

www.skillsforcare.org.uk
www.scie.org.uk

Appendix 1: The Impact Of Increasing Pay Rates In Frontline Social Care

There is no doubt that care workers deserve to be paid more, and that if they were, it would hugely improve the perceived attractiveness of a career in care. A study in the US of the impact when hourly rates were doubled over eighteen months in 2002 tells us that.[94] More recent studies in 2021 by the EU Agency, the European Foundation for the improvement of Living and Working Conditions, reported that wages in long-term care are 21% below average hourly national earnings across the EU, dropping to 31% less than average in the UK.[95]

Low pay is linked to low self-esteem, poor public perception and can lead to burnout as care workers either work longer hours than they would choose to or have to take second jobs to make ends meet.

But more money is by no means the silver bullet for our widening care gap. In fact, it can lure those who are not committed to or suitable for caring for others into the sector, and can cause retention to worsen as those money-seekers discover it is not for them, or you as their employer decide the same thing first. Higher hourly rates do drive increases in the volume of applicants above all other interventions, but once caring people are in post, money is not a big factor in them leaving.

There is evidence from around the world, where meaningful across-the-board pay rises have been given to care workers, that some recipients take the opportunity to reduce their on-the-job hours in favour of a better work–life balance. One of the most studied cases was the New Zealand Pay Equity Settlement of 2017. After the award, 35% of home and community support workers reported they had reduced their hours, with approximately half of those saying it was their decision. Over 52% of New Zealand's care workers surveyed reported having unpaid caring responsibilities for children, disabled or elderly relatives alongside their employment.[96]

Prior to the introduction of first the National Minimum Wage and then the National Living Wage in the UK in 2016, it was the not-for-profit providers and local authorities that commonly offered the most attractive wages and benefits. This differentiator has been eroded as the floor-level hourly rate has been raised. Since this was not applied just to the social care sector, substitute jobs such as retail and hospitality work have maintained their appeal to those whose priority is to earn money.

In local authority-funded social care, there will always be a de facto cap on wages. As the shortage of staff grows and new entrants emerge catering solely to the self-funded market, such as luxury retirement communities and some homecare providers, I expect to see a gradual movement of care workers from state-funded work to better paid roles elsewhere, where they can also spend more quality time with consumers.

There are three concepts to mention that influence the role pay plays in staff turnover. The first is the level of satisfaction the worker has with the pay on offer. Primary breadwinners will likely be less satisfied with their hourly rate than someone who has other sources of income or fewer outgoings.

The second is the concept of pay parity. As an experienced member of the care team, how do I feel about unreliable or inexperienced new starters being paid the same as me? What about NHS staff being paid more for a similar role?

Finally, offering transitional pay to long-serving or specialist employees when they experience a loss of earnings due to a client going into hospital or dying could be valuable in care settings such as live-in care, homecare or supported living. There is a close association with case closings and worker turnover where there is a one-to-one worker–client relationship.

 Tip: Since raising pay rates is often not practical, consider focusing your recruitment on those who are not so fixated on the money. These include active retirees and those attracted by your reputation and culture. However, as we have discussed, there is a risk, in my view, that those with a strong 'calling to care' are being taken advantage of by society at large, or employers, because of their desire to put others before themselves.

 Tip: For homecare and live-in care employers, consider if transitional pay can be offered to experienced staff to avoid any temporary loss of earnings, triggering them to leave.

 Tip: Performance-related pay bonuses that incentivise productivity and improved attendance are likely to be self-funding.

Appendix 2: *I Care...* Ambassadors

Skills for Care's *I Care... Ambassadors* scheme operates across England and its goal is to promote careers in care.

I Care... Ambassadors are care workers who inspire and motivate people to understand more about working in social care. The ambassador role involves workers delivering activities and a talk about what it's like to work in social care in schools, colleges and Job Centres with young people and job seekers. Even though these are two of the tougher potential sources of staff, one in four people said they were more likely to consider a career in the care sector after hearing from an ambassador. Equally importantly, Skills for Care found 83% of care workers felt more motivated in their care role after becoming an ambassador.

For more information, visit the Skills for Care website: www.skillsforcare.org.uk

Appendix 3:
The Legal Issues

Recruitment

There are many legal issues relevant to the recruitment process. James Sage, Employment Partner at RWK Goodman LLP, has identified a few key areas that UK-based organisations involved in the recruitment process need to be aware of.

Immigration issues

There is a duty of employers in the UK to prevent illegal working. Employers should therefore ensure employees have the appropriate right to work in the UK. If employees do not have the right to work in the UK, the employer could be committing a criminal offence and may be liable for a large civil penalty.

Increasing numbers of care providers are recruiting overseas workers to fill job vacancies due to the shortage of UK-based workers. A sponsor licence is required to recruit (i) overseas workers coming to the UK to work, or (ii) overseas workers already in the UK working under the sponsor licence of another employer. Employers holding a sponsor licence must comply with stringent compliance and reporting duties and be prepared for an inspection by the Home Office.

Data protection

The General Data Protection Regulation (GDPR) and Data Protection Act 2018 (DPA 2018) govern the processing of personal data of data subjects, including applicants for employment. Prospective employers who act as data controllers when processing information about candidates, have to comply with these data protection laws throughout, and following, the recruitment process. This includes having an appropriate privacy policy in place for candidates.

Discrimination

Employers have a responsibility to ensure that no unlawful discrimination takes place during the recruitment process. The Equality Act 2010 (EqA 2010) outlaws discrimination, harassment and victimisation in recruitment on the grounds of any of the following protected characteristics: age, disability, gender reassignment, marriage and civil partnership, maternity, pregnancy, race, religion or belief, sex or sexual orientation. Employers must, in particular, be careful not to discriminate: (i) in the recruitment arrangements (including advertising, going through job applications, selecting candidates for interview); (ii) in deciding to whom to offer employment; and (iii) as to the terms on which employment is offered.

While discrimination is generally prohibited, in certain circumstances employers may be able to rely on an exception in the EqA 2010 to justify otherwise discriminatory actions. There are two key exemptions that are likely to apply in the social care sector: occupational requirements and positive action. Occupational requirements are where the employer can show that they need the job to be done by someone with a particular protected characteristic (eg if a female homecare client requests that they receive personal care from a female care worker). Positive action is where the employer can show that persons with a particular protected characteristic are disadvantaged and, in those circumstances, the employer can treat a person with the relevant characteristic more favourably than others, as long as they meet certain requirements set out in the EqA 2010.

Retention

Legally compliant HR management is critical to retaining staff, creating a positive, high-performing and caring workplace culture, and reducing business risk. Managers and leaders must be properly trained in people management and have a good understanding of employment law (or external legal support) and know how to implement internal procedures (such as sickness absence, performance, or grievances/whistleblowing), in a proactive and compliant way.

If you have any queries or comments regarding this Appendix or any legal issues relevant to recruitment or employment, you can contact James Sage, Employment Partner at RWK Goodman LLP, which has a dedicated team of health and social care legal experts.

References

1   LA Lindquist, K Tam, E Friesema and GJ Martin, 'Paid
    caregiver motivation, work conditions, and falls among
    senior clients', *Archives Gerontology Geriatrics*, 55/2 (2012),
    442–445, https://doi.org/10.1016/j.archger.2012.01.008,
    accessed 19 April 2023
2   Office for National Statistics, 'Living longer and old-age
    dependency – what does the future hold?' (Census 2021),
    www.ons.gov.uk/peoplepopulationandcommunity/
    birthsdeathsandmarriages/ageing/articles/
    livinglongerandoldagedependencywhatdoesthe
    futurehold/2019-06-24, accessed 28 March 2023
3   RD Putnam, *Bowling Alone* (Simon & Schuster, 2000)
4   J Jabbal, S Ross, S Bottery, D Maguire and M Martin,
    'Young people in the health and social care workforce'
    (King's Fund, September 2021), www.kingsfund.org.uk/
    sites/default/files/2022-01/Young%20people%20in%20
    health%20and%20care%20workforce%20final.pdf; Skills
    for Care, 'The state of the adult social care workforce in
    England' (21 October 2020), https://careengland.org.uk/
    wp-content/uploads/2020/11/The-state-of-the-adult-
    social-care-sector-and-workforce-2020.pdf, accessed 19
    April 2023

5   Skills for Care, 'The size and structure of the adult
    social care sector and workforce in England' (published
    July 2022), www.skillsforcare.org.uk/adult-social-care-
    workforce-data/Workforce-intelligence/publications/
    national-information/The-size-and-structure-of-the-adult-
    social-care-sector-and-workforce-in-England.aspx, accessed
    28 March 2023

6   Skills for Care, 'The state of the adult social care sector and
    workforce in England' (2021), www.skillsforcare.org.uk/
    adult-social-care-workforce-data/Workforce-intelligence/
    publications/national-information/The-state-of-the-adult-
    social-care-sector-and-workforce-in-England.aspx, accessed
    28 March 2023

7   Office for National Statistics, 'Care homes and estimating
    the self-funding population, England: 2021 to 2022' (Census
    2021), www.ons.gov.uk/peoplepopulationandcommunity/
    healthandsocialcare/socialcare/articles/carehomesande
    stimatingtheselffundingpopulationengland/2021to2022,
    accessed 28 March 2023

8   The Homecare Association, 'Homecare Association
    Minimum Price for Homecare 2023-24' (Homecare
    Association, 2022), www.homecareassociation.org.uk/
    resource/minimum-price-for-homecare-2023-24.html,
    accessed 28 March 2023

9   www.health.org.uk

10 The King's Fund, an independent charity working to
    improve health and care in England, www.kingsfund.org.uk

11 'The state of social care and support provision in England'
    (Care Provider Alliance briefing, November 2022), https://
    careprovideralliance.org.uk/state-of-care-and-support-
    nov-2022-cpa-briefing, accessed 28 March 2023

12 eurofound.europa.eu/publications/article/2021/wages-in-
    long-term-care-and-other-social-services-21-below-average,
    accessed 19 April 2023

13 LA Lindquist, K Tam, E Friesema and GJ Martin, 'Paid
    caregiver motivation, work conditions, and falls among
    senior clients', *Archives Gerontology Geriatrics*, 55/2 (2012),
    442–445, https://doi.org/10.1016/j.archger.2012.01.008,
    accessed 19 April 2023

14 Office for National Statistics, 'Age by single year' (Census
    2021), www.ons.gov.uk/datasets/TS007/editions/2021/
    versions/2/filter-outputs/490fd74e-4d08-4cfe-aa05-
    8b9429182275#get-data, accessed 28 March 2023

15 Office for National Statistics, 'Reasons for workers aged over 50 years leaving employment since the start of the coronavirus pandemic: wave 2' (Census 2021), https://tinyurl.com/mvf39s85, accessed 28 March 2023

16 M Kleiman, *Hire Tough, Manage Easy* (Humetrics Press, 2006)

17 LW Porter and RM Steers, 'Organizational, work, and personal factors in employee turnover and absenteeism', Psychological Bulletin, 80/2 (1973), 151–176

18 E Garla, 'Recruiting with SMS, WhatsApp or simply short texts vs email', www.linkedin.com/pulse/recruiting-sms-whatsapp-simply-short-texts-vs-emails-eugeniu-girla, accessed 19 April 2023

19 J Hunter, 'Testing as a predictor of training success and job performance', Michigan State University

20 S Tweed and D West, 'Top techniques in recruiting top quality caregivers in private duty homecare' (2015), http://leadinghomecare.com/wp-content/uploads/2015/08/2015-Caregiver-Recruiting-Study-Final-PDF.pdf, accessed 19 April 2023

21 LA Lindquist, K Tam, E Friesema and GJ Martin, 'Paid caregiver motivation, work conditions, and falls among senior clients', *Archives Gerontology Geriatrics*, 55/2 (2012), 442–445, https://doi.org/10.1016/j.archger.2012.01.008, accessed 19 April 2023

22 Office for National Statistics 2011, 'Census analysis – distance travelled to work, England and Wales', (26 March 2014) www.ons.gov.uk/peoplepopulationandcommunity/populationandmigration/populationestimates/datasets/2011censusdetailedcharacteristicsontraveltoworkandcarorvanavailabilityforlocalauthoritiesinenglandandwales

23 Data supplied by IQ Timecard, www.uniqueiq.co.uk

24 M Brull, 'Tests improve hiring decisions at Franciscan Health System', *Personnel Journal*, 72/11 (1993), 89–92

25 IH Beardwell and TL Claydon, *Human Resource Management: A contemporary approach*, 4th edition (Prentice Hall, London), adapted from N Anderson and V Shackleton, *Successful Selection Interviewing* (1993)

26 M Mickus, CC Luz and A Hogan, 'Voices from the front: Recruitrment and retention of direct care workers in long-term care across Michigan', Michigan State University (22 April 2004)

27 Data supplied by IQ Timecard, www.uniqueiq.co.uk

28 Sticky People London Homecare no-show evaluation Jan–Mar 2015, https://stickypeople.co.uk

29 MyCNAjobs.com

30 '5 tips to avoid no shows', Cohesion Blog (9 June 2015), https://cohesionrecruitment.com/news/avoid-no-shows, accessed 28 March 2023

31 L Davis, 'The Employee Machine: 57 lock-tight solutions to help you consistently churn out the best hourly employees', www.davisdelany.com/_p/prd14/3365961971/product/ the-employee-machine, accessed 19 April 2023

32 M Kleiman, *Hire Tough, Manage Easy* (Humetrics Press, 2006)

33 Kerry can be reached at kerrycleary.vbaconsulting@gmail.com

34 www.skillsforcare.org.uk

35 Sticky People client data 2015–2017, https://stickypeople.co.uk

36 L Davis, *3 Simple Steps to Getting More Applicants*, ebook available at www.davisdelaney.com

37 S Dixon, 'UK: Facebook audience 2023, by gender', (March 2023) www.statista.com/statistics/1315687/uk-facebook-audience-by-gender/#:~:text=In%20January%20 2023%2C%2053.9%20percent,and%2046.1%20percent%20 were%20men, accessed 28 March 2023

38 Healthcare92, https://socialmedia92.com

39 CMS Direct Service Workforce Demonstration, 'Promising practices in marketing, recruitment and selection interventions' (2006)

40 P Glock, 'Home Health Aide and Homemaker Survey Report', Columbus, OH: Ohio Department of Aging (1995)

41 JobVite Research (2012), www.jobvite.com/collections

42 Carers Trust website (2016), https://carers.org

43 J Livingston, 'Solutions You Can Use: Transforming the long-term care workforce', American Association of Homes and Services for the Aging and the Institute for the Future of Aging Services (2008)

44 S Tweed, Leading Homecare (2005)

45 https://www.ukpetfood.org/information-centre/ statistics/historical-pet-data.html, accessed 19 April 2023

46 Brycelands Removal and Storage, 'Surprising stats about moving in the UK' (March 2017), https://tinyurl. com/45cw7h2t, accessed 28 March 2023

47 Department of Health and Social Care, unpublished research data (2018)

48 S Tweed, Leading Homecare Recruitment Survey 2015

49 Skillsforcare.org.uk

50 Skills for Care, 'The state of the adult social care sector and workforce in England' (October 2022), www.skillsforcare. org.uk/Adult-Social-Care-Workforce-Data/Workforce- intelligence/publications/national-information/The-state- of-the-adult-social-care-sector-and-workforce-in-England. aspx, accessed 28 March 2023

51 Office for National Statistics, 'Annual Population Survey' 2021, https://www.ons.gov.uk/ employmentandlabourmarket/peopleinwork/ employmentandemployeetypes/methodologies/ annualpopulationsurveyapsqmi, accessed 19 April 2023

52 XpertHR Survey 2020, https://www.xperthr.co.uk/survey- analysis/xperthr-benefits-and-allowances-survey-2020- overview/165432, accessed 19 April 2023

53 JK Straker and RC Atchley, 'Recruiting and retaining frontline workers in long-term care: Usual organizational practice in Ohio', Scripps Gerontology Center, Miami University (June 1999)

54 Home Care Pulse Survey 2020, https://www. homecarepulse.com/benchmarking/2020-study, accessed 19 April 2023

55 www.skillsforcare.org.uk/Adult-Social-Care-Workforce- Data/Workforce-intelligence/documents/State-of-the- adult-social-care-sector/The-state-of-the-adult-social-care- sector-and-workforce-2022.pdf, accessed 19 April 2023

56 D Seavey, 'The cost of frontline turnover in long-term care', Better Jobs, Better Care (October 2004), https://leadingage. org/wp-content/uploads/drupal/Cost_Frontline_ Turnover.pdf, accessed 28 March 2023

57 www.bcg.com/publications/2022/address-care-crisis-to- fix-labor-shortage, accessed 19 April 2023

58 JS Dill, JC Morgan and VW Marshall, 'Contingency, employment intentions, and retention of vulnerable low- wage workers: an examination of nursing assistants in nursing homes' *Gerontologist*, 53/2 (2013), 222-34, https:// doi.org/10.1093/geront/gns085, accessed 28 March 2023

59 PH Feldman, AM Sapienza and NM Kane, *Who Cares for Them?: Workers in the home care industry* (Greenwood Press, 1990)

60 www.bcg.com/publications/2022/address-care-crisis-to- fix-labor-shortage, accessed 19 April 2023

61 'In their own words: Pennsylvania's frontline workers in long term care. A report to the Pennsylvania

intra-governmental council on long term care'
(February 2001), www.aging.pa.gov/organization/
PennsylvaniaLongTermCareCouncil/Documents/
Reports/PennsylvaniaIntraGovernmentalCouncilOnLTC/
InTheirOwn%20WordsPennsylvania%E2%80%99s%20
FrontlineWorkersinLongTerm%20CareFebruary2001.pdf,
accessed 19 April 2023

62   Ibid
63   Ibid
64   National Care Forum, Personnel Survey Report 2016,
www.nationalcareforum.org.uk, accessed 23 April 2023
65   MA Zottoli and WP Wanous, 'Recruitment source research:
Current status and future directions', *Human Resources
Management Review*, 10 (2000), 353–382
66   V Mittal, J Rosen, C Leana, 'A dual-driver model of
retention and turnover in the direct care workforce',
Gerontologist, 49/5 (October 2009), 623-34, https://doi.
org/10.1093/geront/gnp054, accessed 28 March 2023
67   C Donoghue, NG Castle, 'Leadership styles of nursing
home administrators and their association with staff
turnover' *Gerontologist*, 49/2, (April, 2009),166-74, https://
doi.org/10.1093/geront/gnp021, accessed 28 March 2023
68   Skills for Care, www.skillsforcare.org.uk/Adult-Social-
Care-Workforce-Data/Workforce-intelligence/documents/
State-of-the-adult-social-care-sector/The-state-of-the-
adult-social-care-sector-and-workforce-2022.pdf, accessed
19 April 2023
69   National Care Forum, Personnel Survey Report 2016,
www.nationalcareforum.org.uk, accessed 23 April 2023
70   RA Baughman and KE Smith, 'Labor mobility of the direct
care workforce: Implications for the provision of long-term
care', *Health Economics*, 21 (2012), 1402–1415
71   Unique:IQ, 'Zero Hours Contracts – An Analysis' (no
date), www.uniqueiq.co.uk/zero-hours-contracts-analysis,
accessed 28 March 2023
72   Skills for Care, 'NMDS trend briefing issue 2 recruitment
and retention'; PHI, 'Workforce strategies no 4, Guaranteed
hours program' PHI paper (2007)
73   J Barratt, 'Recruitment and Selection in the UK Care Sector:
A Longitudinal Study of Effectiveness in Resourcing
Methods and Practice' (July 2019)
74   Adult Social Care: Benchmarking public attitudes to
working in the sector, ORC International commissioned

research on behalf of the Department of Health and Social Care Autumn 2018

75 V Mittal, J Rosen and C Leana, 'A dual-driver model of retention and turnover in the direct care workforce', *Gerontologist*, 49/5 (October 2009), 623–34, https://doi. org/10.1093/geront/gnp054, accessed 28 March 2023

76 G Lloyd, 'Two in five staff have left the care sector as they "didn't feel valued"', *Homecare Insight* (December 2022), www.homecareinsight.co.uk/two-in-five-staff-have-left-the-care-sector-as-they-didnt-feel-valued, accessed 28 March 2023

77 K Pillemer, *Solving the Frontline Crisis in Long-Term Care* (Frontline Publishing Corporation, 1996)

78 Personal conversation

79 PH Feldman, AM Sapienza and NM Kane, *Who Cares for Them?: Workers in the home care industry* (Greenwood Press, 1990)

80 C Donoghue, NG Castle NG, 'Leadership styles of nursing home administrators and their association with staff turnover' *Gerontologist*, 49/2, (April, 2009),166-74, https://doi.org/10.1093/geront/gnp021

81 M West, *Compassionate Leadership: Sustaining wisdom, humanity and presence in health and social care* (The Swirling Leaf Press, 2021)

82 PHI, 'Introducing peer mentoring in long-term care settings', (PHI 2003), www.phinational.org/wp-content/uploads/2017/07/WorkforceStrategies2.pdf, accessed 19 April 2023

83 Phinational.org

84 PHI, 'Workforce strategies no2, Peer mentoring', (PHI 2003), www.phinational.org/wp-content/uploads/2017/07/WorkforceStrategies2.pdf, accessed 19 April 2023

85 Phinational.org

86 PHI, Creating a Culture of Retention: A coaching approach to supervision (PHI September 2001, November 2002, December 2005, November 2008)

87 PACE Central New York Case Study (PHI 2010)

88 Abt Associates, 'Appropriateness of nurse staffing ratios in nursing homes, Phase II Final Report', prepared for the Centers for Medicare and Medicaid Services (Abt Associates 2001), https://theconsumervoice.org/uploads/

files/issues/CMS-Staffing-Study-Phase-II.pdf, accessed 19 April 2023

89   B Franklin and CU Brancati, 'Moved to care: The impact of migration on the adult social care workforce', *Independent Age* (November 2015), www.independentage.org/sites/default/files/2016-05/IA%20Moved%20to%20care%20report_12%2011%2015.pdf, accessed 19 April 2023

90   J Livingston, 'Solutions You Can Use: Transforming the long-term care workforce', American Association of Homes and Services for the Aging and the Institute for the Future of Aging Services (2008), www.ltsscenter.org/resource-library/Solutions_You_Can_Use.pdf, accessed 19 April 2023

91   D Lehman, P Fenza and L Hollinger-Smith, 'Diversity and cultural competency in health care settings: A Mather LifeWays orange paper', www.ecald.com/assets/Resources/Assets/Diversity-and-Cultural-Competency.pdf, accessed 19 April 2023

92   Multiple sources including: SS Butler, M Brennan-Ing, S Wardamasky and A Ashley, 'Determinants of longer job tenure among home care aides: What makes some stay on the job while others leave?', *Journal of Applied Gerontology*, 33 (2014); and 'Older Direct-Care Workers: Key Facts and Trends January 2014' PHI New York; and PH Feldman, AM Sapienza and NM Kane, *Who Cares for Them?: Workers in the home care industry* (Greenwood Press, 1990)

93   'In their own words: Pennsylvania's frontline workers in long term care. A report to the Pennsylvania intra-governmental council on long term care' (February 2001) www.aging.pa.gov/organization/PennsylvaniaLongTermCareCouncil/Documents/Reports/PennsylvaniaIntraGovernmentalCouncilOnLTC/InTheirOwn%20WordsPennsylvania%E2%80%99s%20FrontlineWorkersinLongTerm%20CareFebruary2001.pdf, accessed 19 April 2023

94   C Howes, 'Living wages and retention of homecare workers in San Francisco' (Department of Economics, Connecticut College, June 2004), https://digitalcommons.conncoll.edu/cgi/viewcontent.cgi?article=1001&context=econfacpub, accessed 19 April 2023

95   H Dubois, 'Wages in long-term care and other social services 21% below average' (Eurofound, March 2021), www.eurofound.europa.eu/publications/article/2021/

wages-in-long-term-care-and-other-social-services-21-below-average, accessed 28 March 2023

96   K Ravenswood and J Douglas, 'The impact of the Pay Equity Settlement: Data from the 2019 Care Workforce Survey', NZ Work Research Institute (2022), https://workresearch.aut.ac.nz/__data/assets/pdf_file/0004/628681/Pay-Equity-Report-2022.pdf, accessed 28 March 2023

Acknowledgements

I continue to learn so much from all those I meet and speak to in social care and healthcare in the UK, Ireland, mainland Europe, the US and Australia. It's not possible to list everyone, because I would surely miss key people out, but you all know who you are.

Particular thanks go to my late parents, the Reverend Christopher and Maisie Eastwood, who brought me up never to forget that caring for others is at the heart of a civilised society.

The Author

Neil Eastwood is a UK-based speaker, commentator and adviser on best practice frontline care worker recruitment and retention. He publishes blogs, articles and videos as well as presenting on this topic around the world. His findings and recommendations have generated dramatic workforce improvements across a wide range of care providers.

He has spent many years studying every aspect of how to find, select and keep those who are paid to care for others and what we can learn from the best care employers around the world. Previously he was a director at a 10,000-staff care provider and before that worked in the healthcare sector.

He is the founder and CEO of Care Friends Ltd, the employee referral app for the social care sector operated in partnership with Skills for Care. The app is widely used by employers across the UK and Australia and was the recipient of the prestigious King's Award for Enterprise for Innovation in 2023.

Neil studied at Plymouth University, the University of Sheffield and then Harvard Business School and holds a First-Class Combined Honours Degree in social science, and an MBA. As a vicar's son, he was brought up in an environment where supporting the vulnerable in society was always prioritised over personal gain. Hopefully, some of this rubbed off.

Saving Social Care was written to help care providers meet the growing demands for high-quality care and, through them, reach out to the hundreds of thousands of people in all walks of life who have yet to discover how personally fulfilling paid care work can be. It is in its second edition.

Finally...

Please visit www.savingsocialcare.com to access our whiteboard videos and blog.

Neil regularly speaks at care and healthcare conferences and manager forums in the UK, Australia and further afield, and hopes to meet you at a future event. Please do give your feedback and share your own experiences.

Connect with Neil on:

in www.linkedin.com/in/neileastwood

@StickyNeil

Printed in Great Britain
by Amazon

27030662R00188